PRIDE OF
OUR PEOPLE

Other books by David C. Gross

English-Hebrew, Hebrew-English
Conversational Dictionary

How to Be Jewish

The Jewish People's Almanac

1,001 Questions and Answers
About Judaism

A Justice for All the People:
Louis D. Brandeis

Pictorial History of the Jewish People
by Nathan Ausubel (Updated)

One Hundred Children
by Lena Kuchler-Silberman
(Edited and Translated)

The Hunter
by Tuvia Friedman
(Edited and Translated)

Love Poems from the Hebrew
(Edited)

Dictionary of the Jewish Religion
by Ben Isaacson(Edited)

PRIDE OF
OUR PEOPLE

A New Selection of 36 Life Stories of Outstanding, Contemporary Jewish Men and Women

by

DAVID C. GROSS

WALKER AND COMPANY

New York

For my children, and their children

First Large Print Edition published by
Walker Publishing Company, Inc., 1991.

Published simultaneously in Canada by
Thomas Allen & Son Canada, Limited, Markham, Ontario.

Library of Congress Cataloging-in-Publication Data

Gross, David C. 1923–
Pride of our people: a new selection of 36 life stories of outstanding, contemporary Jewish men and women /
by David C. Gross.
p.   cm.
ISBN 0-8027-2648-8
1. Jews—Biography.   I. Title.
DS115.G72   1991
920'.0092924—dc20   90-38087
CIP

Printed in the United States of America

2 4 6 8 10 9 7 5 3 1

Contents

PREFACE

WE LIVE IN AN AGE with few heroic personalities—men and women whose lives are proof positive of the great heights to which a mortal person can reach. On all sides we see the overwhelming materialist philosophy that has engulfed the world, leading many people to become cynical and deeply suspicious of the eternal truths taught by all great religious movements.

The Jewish people in particular are wary of "great figures." Comparisons inevitably arise between someone who is said to be a "great personality" and those revered figures who have become part and parcel of Jewish tradition, whose lives and works have been taught and expounded on— the incomparable biblical personalities, and the handful of outstanding people who made their mark on Jewish history in postbiblical days. These were selfless, dedicated men and women, and comparisons with modern newcomers invariably lead to a feeling of dubiousness.

Today, most Jews approach the rabbis in the community with an innate sense of respect and honor, sometimes even awe, and when it turns out that a spiritual leader is after all a human being like everyone else, heads are shaken, and one hears, "Of course, I could have told you so."

And yet there are truly heroic Jewish figures in our time, and if we do not know about them, it is precisely because part of their greatness lies in the fact that they eschew personal publicity. To perform the *mitzvah*, the good deed prescribed in Jewish teaching, that is the crux of the matter. To seek out recognition and honor is to negate the good deed itself.

In almost every generation of Jewish history— stretching back to the days of Abraham and right up to our own day—there have been many thousands of exemplary Jewish men and women whose lives served to inspire young and old.

In attempting to cover a cross section of thirty-six such biographical sketches, I have had to winnow down the list to a select number, whose lives and achievements would form a cohesive pattern of people who attained prominence in their respective fields of endeavor and who simultaneously remained dedicated, committed members, and often leaders, of the Jewish community.

The areas of endeavor encompassed include science and government, education and politics, art and entertainment, industry and scholarship, literature and religion, social service and medicine.

One additional category is included, one that is difficult to define. And that is the self-sacrificial heroism of men and women who gave their all to help rescue or at least bring succor to their fellow Jews who in the course of the past half century faced death and destruction at the hands of the Nazis.

The lives of great men and women often serve to help mold the still malleable minds and hearts of young people. It is my earnest hope that the exemplary lives of the men and women portrayed in this volume will help fashion the future of a new generation of Jewish young people.

D.C.G.

Jonas Salk
The Man Who Conquered Polio

NOWADAYS NEARLY EVERY child is inoculated with the Salk antipolio vaccine as a routine measure. But prior to 1955 there was no such vaccine, and tens of thousands of children and many adults were afflicted with this dread killer that crippled limbs and seemed to have no cure. The world still remembers the appearance of President Franklin D. Roosevelt, who contracted polio as an adult and spent the rest of his life in a chair, unable to walk without steel braces and the help of others.

Jonas Salk was born in New York in 1914 and, like most boys, concentrated on baseball, although he was early acknowledged to be an exceptional student. He was admitted to the City College of New York at the age of fifteen, planning to become

1

a lawyer. To broaden his background, he also enrolled in a science course, and quickly realized that this was where his real interests lay.

He was accepted at the medical school of New York University and decided that he would devote himself to medical research, and within a matter of years he was instrumental in developing vaccines against the flu. The great scourge of polio remained a challenge to every research-minded scientist, and Dr. Salk wanted to see if he could find a preventative.

When the University of Pittsburgh asked him to set up a special virus laboratory, he accepted, and for the next eight years he devoted nearly every hour to seeking a vaccine against the dread disease. Colleagues said he worked twenty hours a day, every day of the week, as he tried one formulation after another to discover the vaccine that would work. After discovering what he felt was the suitable vaccine, he knew it still had to be tested on human beings, and used both himself and his own children for the experimental injections. The first results were encouraging, and he then proceeded to test more vaccinations with additional numbers of people. In 1955 he announced to a startled and grateful world that he had found the vaccine that would prevent polio. It was a milestone in medical annals, and a day thankful parents would always remember.

The vaccine was named for him, and has become a potent preventative against the feared disease among tens of millions of people. He received honors and awards from many governments and institutions, including the Presidential Citation and the Congressional Medal for Distinguished Achievement.

After serving for a number of years as a consultant on viruses to the United Nations World Health Organization, he established the Salk Institute for Biological Studies at La Jolla, California, of which he is the director. One of the targets of the research specialists gathered at that center is the conquest of at least some forms of cancer.

Salk has visited Israel frequently, lecturing to university and medical groups and expressing his admiration for the high quality of medical research that is being carried out there.

For a number of years, Salk has been experimenting to find a cure for AIDS, the often fatal disease that has claimed tens of thousands of lives. In 1990, the Food and Drug Administration approved nationwide testing of a new possible cure, tentatively known as the Salk immunogen. Among the volunteers who will test the new AIDS-prevention vaccine is Jonas Salk, who tested the then new polio vaccine on himself, back in 1955.

SIMON WIESENTHAL
The Nazi Hunter

In 1933 ADOLF HITLER took power in Germany and launched the Nazi era, which ended only in 1945, after the defeat of Germany and its allies in one of history's bloodiest wars, World War II. During that period of a dozen years, which saw hundreds of thousands of soldiers from practically all European countries, the United States, and Japan killed and wounded, a horrible event took place that to this day people find difficult to understand: the deliberate extermination of six million Jews in Europe, who represented fully one third of the world's Jewish community. The disaster has come to be known as the Holocaust.

One of the pitifully small number of Jews who survived the Nazi concentration camps is a man named Simon Wiesenthal. Like so many other survivors of the Nazi era, he lost his family as well as his interest in resuming his profession as an architect after the war ended. A man of indomitable will, he established a small office in Vienna for the sole purpose of tracking down every man and woman who had been a Nazi war criminal and bringing them to justice.

There were those who said it was a hopeless task and that finding the Nazis would be impossible. Others urged him to concentrate on the future and try to rebuild his life. But Wiesenthal reasoned otherwise: He said that the Nazis had to be punished so that no such system of pure evil could ever be allowed to develop again. He said also that allowing them to live without punishment,without justice taking its course, would hand them a victory over the Jews and the other people they had massacred, and that must not be allowed to happen.

In the course of nearly forty years, with the support of volunteers from all parts of the world who share his feelings about letting unrepentant Nazis get off scot free, he has tracked down more than three thousand Nazi criminals, of whom more than a third have been brought to trial, the vast majority of whom have been convicted and punished. One of the most notorious of these was Adolf Eichmann, who was kidnapped by Israeli agents and brought to Jerusalem where he was put on trial, with millions of people able to view the proceedings via television.

New Nazi groups have offered to pay one

million marks to anyone who would assassinate Wiesenthal. His Documentation Center in Vienna and the invaluable files it contains are carefully guarded around the clock, and Wiesenthal himself always travels with an armed guard. He does not lightly dismiss any of the modern versions of Nazi organizations that have sprung up in various countries, including the United States.

His office in Vienna is now collecting samples of Nazi-type hate publications that call for assaults against Jews and other minority groups, and, wherever and whenever he can, he urges government authorities to quash these groups at once. They are based, he explains, on expressions of racial and religious hatred, on sentiments that proclaim the superiority of one group over another, and on the ambitions of evil men who are willing to exploit unrest, discontent and disturbed people's frustrations for their own benefit.

Wiesenthal is especially sensitive about the United States which he admires and looks up to as the model of all free nations He remembers that although he now weighs two hundred pounds he was a skeletal ninety pounds when American forces liberated him toward the end of the Second World War. The United State must outlaw all hate groups, he insists, because it is "the only way to protect innocent people from indoctrinated crazies."

Wiesenthal has been lecturing to college organizations and many other Jewish and non-Jewish groups, but he realizes that he is already past seventy and he does not have much time left to press his hunt for Nazis. He has said that the "Nazis I hunt down are not the problem anymore—they want to live out the rest of their lives in peace, and I hunt them down only because they committed crimes and must be punished.

"The real problem of today are the Nazis who have been indoctrinated by Nazi philosophy. We must find a method of undoing their indoctrination."

There is no doubt that so long as he is able to, Wiesenthal will continue his virtually one-man battle against Nazis, both those of the past and those of today and tomorrow.

NATHAN STRAUS
Milk for All the People

MILK, THAT WONDERFUL, all-purpose food that helps infants and small children grow into healthy adults, is something taken for granted by most people—but it was not too long ago that it was spreading disease rather than encouraging health, and therein lies the story of a modest, determined Jew who had come to the United States as a small child, attained great wealth, and used almost all of it for the performance of good deeds, among them the transformation of milk into the vital food it has become for millions upon millions of people throughout the world.

Nathan Straus was born in 1848 in Germany and was brought to the United States as a small boy. After living at first in the South, he and his family moved to New York, where he soon found work in a store. Ambitious and studious, young Nathan studied bookkeeping after working hours, and eventually became the store's chief bookkeeper. In the course of time he became a partner in the great Macy's department stores, and began to build his fortune.

In the latter part of the nineteenth century, the Lower East Side area of New York City was a major center for immigrants, many of them Jews, all of them poor, many just managing to keep body and soul together, living in firetrap slums. Straus had heard about conditions in the area, but it was only after he paid a personal visit there that he realized how awful were the lives of the people who were forced to live in that neighborhood. He was a man of great compassion for the poor and he made up his mind to try to help. When he learned that one of the greatest problems besetting the immigrants was the death of small infants, apparently because they were being fed contaminated milk, he knew that he had to do something about it.

Across the ocean, in France, the brilliant scientist Louis Pasteur had announced that he knew what it was in milk that caused small children to become ill and die, and he had devised a method of preventing this terrible scourge. What must seem perfectly simple and logical to people nowadays was scoffed at when Pasteur first proposed it— heating the milk and maintaining it at high enough temperature for a given period to kill the germs in it, then letting it cool, and packing the precious fluid in sterilized containers. Strange as it may seem, people laughed at Pasteur, including many physicians, some of whom claimed that since the French scientist was not even a medical doctor, he could not know anything of disease.

But in New York the department store owner Nathan Straus was convinced that Pasteur was right and everyone who mocked him was wrong. He took leave of his business, sailed for France, and, after studying at first hand the Pasteur method of sterilization, hurried back to the United States to introduce the new method to American milk producers.

The processors of milk were outraged by Straus, and attacked him for meddling in their business. His pleas that impure milk was killing thousands of babies were ignored. Straus thereupon established a network of health stations, where he sold pasteurized milk to the people who lived in New York's poor section at less than the cost of producing it, making up the difference from his own funds.

The "milk battle" between Straus and the milk-industry leaders continued for a number of years, but after a while it became clear to everyone that the children who were being raised on pasteurized milk were not falling sick, while those who were drinking the untreated milk continued to grow sick and die.

Gradually various government agencies became

involved in the dispute, and soon one city after another, and eventually most of the world, ordered all milk to be pasteurized before it was sold to the public. Straus had won his battle, in the course of which he saved the lives of countless numbers of babies. New York was so grateful to him that in 1898 he was named president of the Board of Health.

The profound satisfaction that he had received from his work in the milk situation encouraged him to expand his nonprofit chain of stores for the poor, and now he added coal and regular food staples for the needy at prices below what they cost him.

A few years later he established the first tuberculosis-prevention center for children. When a worldwide conference dedicated to the protection of infants took place in Berlin in 1909, the President of the United States sent Straus to lead the American delegation. In the course of World War I, when news reports of the terrible suffering of hundreds of thousands of Jews in eastern Europe reached the United States, he personally donated one hundred thousand dollars for relief work—a sum comparable to at least a million dollars today.

After the end of the war, as tens of thousands of Jews began to arrive in Palestine to lay the groundwork for what is today the State of Israel, Nathan Straus became vitally interested in the pioneering work going on there. He announced his support for the Zionist goal and, after visiting Palestine, set up health stations, milk depots, and schools there. Before he died in 1931, at the age of eighty-three, he had given away more than two thirds of his vast fortune to many projects in Palestine. In his honor and memory the coastal city of Nathanya, north of Tel Aviv, bears his name.

Straus believed firmly each person had a responsibility to leave the world a better place than when he arrived on the scene. By his persuading people to use sterilized milk and by his large gifts for health and education in Palestine and the example he set for all people of means, he left a name that is always recalled with respect, admiration, and love.

Isaac Bashevis Singer
Storyteller to the World

HIS NOVELS AND STORIES have been translated into many languages, and even though Isaac Bashevis Singer writes in Yiddish and concentrates on the life of the Jewish *shtetl* that no longer exists, he has succeeded in creating a vast audience of readers eager for every word he puts to paper. In 1978 he received the Nobel Prize in literature, for which he had been nominated by the famed critic Edmund Wilson; and Rebecca West, herself one of the leading authors of the day, has said that he is the greatest living contemporary writer.

Sophisticated readers of The New Yorker magazine, lovers of literature in Japan, Germany, Israel, Brazil, and many other countries, Jews and non-Jews alike, have found that reading a Singer story or novel is an experience unlike any other. With great skill, almost magically, he succeeds in a few swift strokes of his pen in portraying the character and personality of a man, a woman, a child, in circumstances that are often quite foreign to most of his readers, and manages to keep his readers' interest at almost fever pitch. Many critics have explained his worldwide following as his uncanny ability to tell a story about an individual in terms that are immediately universal. A small, frail man in his seventies with a rosy complexion and an almost entirely bald head, he is a gentle, highly sensitive, and skeptical chronicler of an era and a society that no longer exist but that still contain a vibrant message for modern readers.

Singer was born in a small town near Warsaw, Poland, the son and grandson of rabbis, and for a while was himself a rabbinical student. He worked in his youth as a newspaper translator, proofreader, and reporter, all the time reading, observing, listening to people, and preparing himself for a career as a storyteller.

To Singer, literature must be first and foremost a good story and although he insists that he has no great social or political messages to convey through his work, readers have written him to say that he has helped them to see life anew after they had become deeply discouraged. His narratives blend a sometimes pessimistic view of life with a lyrical belief that "that's the way life is—and you might as well get used to it."

Singer left Poland in the mid-1930s and came to

the United States, explaining that he could see the threat of war and destruction years before the Nazis launched World War II. For many years he labored at his Yiddish writing to earn a modest living, supported by his second wife, who held down a sales job in a New York store. (Singer's first wife, an avowed Communist, took their son to Russia, and eventually settled in Israel. At least once a year Singer travels to Israel to visit his son and grandchildren, who live on a kibbutz.)

Singer has always had profound interest in the supernatural and he believes that in decades to come science will unearth concrete information about extrasensory perception and what is to day called the occult, making these areas respectable subjects for serious study. He considers himself a religious man; although he is not observant of Jewish ritual, he says, "Whenever I am in trouble, I pray. And since I'm always in trouble, I pray a lot."

Over the years his work has been translated into English, and as his knowledge of his adopted language has expanded, he has worked more closely than ever with his translators to ensure just the right word and phrase. He has also become a popular lecturer and frankly enjoys the lecture circuit, since it gives him an opportunity to meet people, and this, he says, is his greatest hobby and nourishment—getting to know people, imagining what they are really like, and sooner or later incorporating this information into his writing. About half of the material in his stories, he admits, is more or less autobiographical.

Singer says that when he writes a story, he does so to satisfy himself and does not think of his readers—explaining that his first readers in Yiddish are older, East European Jews who read the *Jewish Daily Forward*, a Yiddish newspaper, while subsequent readers in translation could be American college professors or Japanese housewives. "A book," he maintains, "is not [the author's] private property. Everybody can find in it what he finds; [it] has an independent kind of life."

The author lives on New York's teeming West Side, and despite the absence of many fellow Yiddish writers in the area, he finds the ambience of the city a constant challenge and source of wonder. He has become deeply attached to America, where he has lived for more than forty years. "My Jewishness is of great importance to me, but I really feel that I am a longtime American and this is my country. I belong to those writers who are grateful to their adopted country."

He maintains an intense interest in Israel and is hopeful for that country's future. "The hatred of Israel is a neurosis," he says. "Things may look bad [for Israel], but in our history things look bad all the time, and we have outlived scores of nations. We Jews have been living in an eternal, permanent crisis."

In recent years Singer has become a vegetarian and only regrets that he did not give up eating meat and fish at an earlier date. He explains that the idea of killing another creature in order to eat it is diametrically opposite to the inner, humane spirit that rests in each person.

Singer loves to spend his mornings in bed, writing for hours in a notebook, and in the afternoons he edits some of his earlier work or transcribes on a battered Yiddish typewriter. Watching him set down word after word on paper, his blue eyes shining with genuine pleasure as he does so, one remembers that he.often writes about a dybbuk, a foreign spirit that has entered a person's body, for he too seems at the moment possessed and obsessed by a power stronger than himself.

GOLDA MEIR
The Lady Prime Minister

CONSIDERED ONE of the outstanding Jewish women of the century and admired by Jews and non-Jews alike for her sincerity, forthrightness, and courage, Golda Meir became a legend in her own lifetime.

She was best known as one of the few women in the world who have directed the destiny of a sovereign country, in her case, as Prime Minister of Israel. In Israel and among Jews in all parts of the world she was known affectionately simply by her first name—she has had such a strong impact on her people that there is really only one Golda in the twentieth century.

She was born Golda Mabovich in Kiev, Russia, in 1898, the daughter of a carpenter. The Jewish communities of czarist Russia were still being subjected to pogroms. Golda Meir has often recalled the impression made on her, when she saw her father boarding up the modest house they occupied in order to keep out bands of hooligans who preyed on defenseless Jewish families.

At the age of eight she came to Milwaukee with her family, where she grew up and graduated from a local teachers' training school. As a teenager, hearing of the anti-Jewish massacres that accompanied the Bolshevik Revolution in 1917, she made up her mind that the answer to the "Jewish problem" was Zionism, especially the Socialist version that she felt would guarantee a decent life for all classes of people.

Life in Milwaukee was incomparably better than what the family had known in Russia. Golda's father was employed in the city's railroad yard, and her mother augmented the family income by operating a dairy store. Through her formative years Golda helped her mother and also found time to develop friendships with some of the neighborhood girls, with whom she was to maintain lifetime ties.

She always excelled in her studies, although years later she admitted that helping her mother run the family store put an extra burden on her which she resented since it often made her late for class. Her older sister, a confirmed Socialist, refused to help out on principle; she wanted to have nothing to do with a capitalist enterprise.

Her early interest in her fellow men and women

was evident even when she was a young student. When she learned that some of the poorer students could not afford to buy the required textbooks, she organized a fund-raising event, inviting the wealthier students and their parents, as well as other people in the neighborhood—and solicited those present for funds to aid the needy students. People opened their pocketbooks and contributed, an event that made Golda's parents beam with pride. At the time, she was all of twelve.

A family crisis ensued when Golda, at the age of fourteen, refused to terminate her studies, as her parents expected her to do. She was determined to get much more education, a demand that her parents could not understand, having come from a society where most girls received even less education than Golda had already obtained. Determined to have her way, Golda fled home and went to live with her sister's family in Denver for a year and a half, until her parents finally relented and agreed to let her go on with her education.

She continued her schooling in Milwaukee, including attending an afternoon Jewish school which was supposed to teach Hebrew but where she wound up learning more Yiddish than the biblical language. Life in the Mabovich household was always exciting, since Golda's mother kept an "open sofa" in the living room for itinerant visitors; these were likely to be visiting lecturers who disdained the Milwaukee hotels, or early Socialist preachers, or distant relatives on their way to new homes in various parts of the United States.

During World War I Golda helped her father, who was involved in an organization seeking to provide aid to Jews in Europe who were caught in the war zones. Around this time, she began to deliver public lectures, often in Yiddish, usually at literary gatherings.

Soon after the war ended in 1918, Golda made up her mind that as a Zionist she belonged in Palestine, helping to fashion a new homeland. "I loved America," she has said, "but I couldn't understand how one could be a Zionist without going to Palestine."

At the age of nineteen she married Morris Myerson, a fellow Socialist, but only on condition that he would agree to go with her to Palestine. Myerson was not a Zionist, but he agreed to her condition. In May 1921 Golda, her husband, and her sister Sheine and two children sailed for Palestine on a barely seaworthy vessel that took fifty-four days to cross the seas. The group arrived in Jaffa in July, by train from Alexandria, Egypt, because Arabs were then rioting in Palestine and refused to allow Jewish passengers arriving by sea to disembark.

The first years in Palestine were incredibly hard for the small party of newcomers, although Golda has written that life on the kibbutz for her at least was one of the finest periods in her life. In the course of time, she became known in the fledgling labor movement in Palestine as a potentially effective woman leader and was persuaded to give up the kibbutz life and devote her energies to the Histadrut, the small but growing national labor confederation.

The confidence that the early Zionist leaders had in her was soon justified, and by 1928 she had become head of the Working Women's Council, and six years later, after a two-year stint raising funds in the United States, she was invited to become a member of the executive of the Histadrut. She began to play an increasingly important role in the political activities of the Histadrut right through the 1940s. In 1946, when the British Mandatory authorities arrested practically all the leaders of the Jewish community in Palestine, she became the acting head of the Jewish Agency's political department, in effect the community's official representative to the British.

There have been many dramatic moments in Golda's life and two that stand out are the fund-raising trip she made to the United States early in 1948, four months before the proclamation of Israeli statehood, and a trip she made in disguise to the king of Jordan four days before Israel's independence was announced.

On her trip to the United States, Golda visited a number of Jewish communities, telling them that the Holocaust in which six million Jews had perished would have been in vain if Israel were not established to make a haven for the survivors and for any other Jews who would require a refuge in the future. By her eloquence and candor she helped raise tens of millions of dollars that were desperately needed at the time, since thousands of Jewish refugees were streaming into Palestine despite the official ban on immigration imposed by the British Mandatory authorities.

Her trip to Amman to see King Abdullah and plead with him to stay out of any war that might follow on the heels of an Israeli announcement of independence was filled with great personal risk. She managed to talk with the king, who in effect told her that he would like to abide by her wishes and stay out of any fighting that might take place, but it was a matter of "honor" or "fate" and he could not do so. Nevertheless, he saw to it that she returned safely to the Israeli side of the border.

She was named the Israeli ambassador to Moscow in 1948, and her arrival in the Soviet capital is credited with the early demonstrations by Russian Jews demanding to be allowed to join their coreligionists abroad. Later she served as Minister of Labor and as Foreign Minister, and in the latter role she became known for her tough, yet sincere addresses at the United Nations, where she offered to establish peaceful relations with any Arab nation willing to sit down with Israel and negotiate a treaty.

As Foreign Minister, she toured many African countries and helped to forge strong bonds of friendship with several developing nations. Photographs of her teaching black women in remote villages how to dance the Israeli *hora* were printed in newspapers around the world. In 1969, following the death of Levi Eshkol, Golda Meir became the fourth Prime Minister of Israel, a post she held until 1974.

One of the most painful moments for her was the decision she reached to step down as Prime Minister in the aftermath of the Yom Kippur War of 1973. Although the war began with an attack by Egypt and Syria, many Israeli leaders blamed themselves for having been unprepared for such an event. The high loss of life in that war and the subsequent drop in morale among most Israelis led her to decide to resign, although she personally had never been accused of having made any wrong decisions with regard to the outbreak or conduct of the war.

She was regarded in Israel as an elder states-woman to whom young and aspiring politicians came with their problems. A Broadway play featuring the noted actress Anne Bancroft opened in New York in 1977, depicting her remarkable life story. Aptly, it was titled simply *Golda*.

Toward the end of 1978, at the age of eighty, she died in a Jerusalem hospital. Leading world figures voiced their admiration for her lifetime of achievement. Perhaps one of the most poignant messages of condolence came from the President of Egypt, Anwar Sadat, who said, "I received with sorrow the news of Mrs. Meir's death. I must, for the sake of history, praise her as an honest foe during the situation of confrontation between us, which we all hope is over forever."

MENDELE
MOCHER SEFARIM
Grandfather of Yiddish Literature

HIS REAL NAME was Shalom Abramovich, but he became known during his lifetime by his pen name, Mendele Mocher Sefarim, or "Mendele the Bookseller." Today he is acknowledged as the grandfather of modern Yiddish literature and one of the truly great figures of modern Jewish writing.

He was born in a typical Russian shtetl in 1835, received an excellent Jewish and general education, and began to write both in Hebrew and Yiddish at an early age. Life became difficult for him when, at the age of thirteen, he lost his father. While still in his teens, he became a schoolteacher with a strong desire to help his people.

In the middle of the nineteenth century the vast majority of the Jews of the world lived in czarist Russia. Their life was harsh, for they were not allowed, without special permission, to leave certain defined areas reserved for them. Most of the Jews were extremely poor; few had an opportunity to advance themselves through education; and the fear of pogroms and attacks was always uppermost in people's minds.

Although he preferred to write in Hebrew and to revive the ancient language of the Jewish people, Mendele set about also to write books and plays in Yiddish that would show his fellow Jews that their only salvation lay in obtaining a better education for themselves and their children and in correcting the weaknesses that existed within the Jewish community itself. Although he was not a socialist nor a Zionist, and in fact the terms were not even known for most of his working life, he has been hailed as one of the early forerunners of both movements. Mendele saw himself as a man with the gift of writing, and he was determined to use it to encourage and uplift his people, who were then passing through a period of despair and hopelessness.

In his writings he stressed the importance of eliminating the corrupt practices that had dominated the Jewish communities for many years and of giving the great majority of the Jews an opportunity to decide on their own affairs. He also believed that the Jews should form alliances with outside political movements that would help to improve their lot in life. On the one hand, he fought the exploitation of the Jewish masses by groups of corrupt leaders who had been in control of their lives for many years, and on the other hand, he urged the Jews to turn away from superstition and join the modern forces of enlightenment that had begun to emerge in western Europe. He also urged them to fight against the tyranny of the Russian regime.

All this he did through his novels, plays, and articles. Because he chose to write in Yiddish in order to reach as wide an audience as possible, his books were enjoyed by large numbers of simple Jews, who sensed in his writing a deep love for the Jewish people and saw in him a champion who sincerely tried to help them out of their difficult lives.

Although he was not a political revolutionary, his books foreshadowed events that were to take place in coming years, including the co-operation of the oppressed Jews and the equally oppressed non-Jewish peasants and workers, all of whom endured great suffering under the regime of the hated czarist government.

He wrote that the anti-Jewish pogroms were nothing less than wars, and asked how it was possible for the instigators of such wars, the pogromists, not only to be let off free for their actions but even to be rewarded by forced payments of ransom by the Jews to prevent any further outbreaks of violence.

31

Many writers in Israel today attribute to Mendele the creation, almost singlehandedly, of the school of realistic writing that evolved in Hebrew in the last half century. And many literary critics describe Mendele as one of the truly great Jewish writers of the century and regret the fact that his work has not become as well known in English and other languages as that of other Jewish authors.

As a young man he also wrote books about nature and popular science, which were a great innovation for Jewish readers of the time. He traveled extensively, from one shtetl to another, always studying the ways of life of the Jews and observing how they and their non-Jewish neighbors got along. One of his most cherished ambitions was to translate the prayer book into Yiddish, but he never fulfilled this idea. He died in 1917, having seen the onset of the Russian Revolution and the early beginnings of the Zionist movement, both of which he hoped would bring an end to Jewish suffering.

ANNE FRANK
Unstilled Voice of the Holocaust

MILLIONS OF PEOPLE have read *The Diary of a Young Girl* or seen the film based on it, *The Diary of Anne Frank*. It is a moving account by a young Jewish girl who hid out with her family and several other Jewish people for two years, from 1942 to 1944, in a "secret annex," actually part of a warehouse belonging to her father, until the Nazis discovered them and sent them to a concentration camp. The *Diary* made it possible for millions of people to understand what the Nazi regime in Europe was really like and to grasp the great suffering that befell the Jewish communities in those countries seized by the Nazis.

Anne was born in Frankfurt, Germany, in 1929. When she was four, her parents took her and her sister, Margot, to Holland, for by then the Nazi regime had already come to power in Germany and the situation for the Jews looked very bleak. After World War II broke out in 1939, six million Jews were deliberately massacred by the Nazi authorities.

The Jewish community in Holland, which was overrun in 1940, did not suffer as much as Jews in other countries, at least in the beginning, because so many Dutch people were violently opposed to the barbaric ideas of the Nazis. But by 1942 the situation had become grim for the Jews, and the Frank family decided to hide out, hoping that the danger of the Nazi era would pass soon.

They moved into a secret part of a commercial building, together with another family, and later were joined by an older man—Jews in great danger of being arrested and deported to their death for no reason other than the fact that they were Jewish. Five devoted friends of the Frank family made it possible for the secret hiding place to succeed for a period of more than two years. These five non-Jewish men and women brought food, clothes, medicines, newspapers to the self-confined residents of the virtual prison, and sustained their hopes that the ordeal would soon come to an end.

When she entered the secret annex, Anne was about thirteen, a talented, sensitive girl who, together with her sister, had received a secondary Jewish education and who understood that, hard as it was for them to remain in hiding, things on the outside were far worse for other Jews, who were being rounded up and brutally murdered every day in every part of the European continent controlled by the Nazis.

She began to keep a diary, and in it she recorded her own observations of the impact of the close quarters in which her own family and the others lived for so long a period. She wrote of human weaknesses, including her own mother's standard of values; of the growing feelings of teen-age infatuation that she began to develop for young Peter, the son of the Van Daan family who lived with the Franks; of her own ambitions to survive the terrible ordeal that they were all passing through and to try to become a writer, a calling for which she believed she had a special talent.

Strangely, despite the conditions of their lives, Anne Frank retained a hopeful outlook on life and expressed her essential confidence in the decency of most people. She wrote that she hoped to live to see the day when the terrible nightmare of the Jewish people would come to an end and a time of peace and universal brotherhood would prevail.

In August of 1944, less than a year before the Nazis surrendered to the Allied forces, the hiding place was discovered and all of its occupants were sent to a death camp. Anne's father, Otto, survived. Two of the Gentile friends of the family who had helped them carry on for two years discovered Anne's diary when they went to inspect the site of the secret hiding place. It was published in 1947 in

Dutch, and later appeared in many other languages, as well as in stage and film versions.

In the Nazi drive to annihilate all Jews, six million perished, among them more than one million children. Anne Frank, sixteen years old when she met her death, was one of the victims, but her name lives on, for through her diary she succeeded in making millions of people understand what happened to the Jewish people, by recounting the lives of eight Jewish men and women locked up for two years in a hiding place in a business building. In her diary Anne Frank wrote:

I want to go on living even after my death. And therefore I am grateful to God for giving me this gift, this possibility of developing myself and of writing, of expressing all that is in me.

ALBERT A. MICHELSON
America's First Nobel Laureate

HE WAS BORN in a small village in Germany in 1852, brought to the United States at the age of two, and grew up first in Nevada and later in San Francisco. At the age of seventeen, alone and without funds or support from government or political figures, Albert Abraham Michelson made the long journey on the newly inaugurated railroad from California to Washington, D.C., to try for an appointment to the U. S. Naval Academy at Annapolis. The son of poor parents, he knew that he had no other way of obtaining a higher education.

Annapolis at first turned him down, although his high school grades were excellent. He was told there was no vacancy. But Michelson was anything but a quitter: He went to the White House, asking for an appointment to see the President, and eventually President Ulysses Grant did see the young man from far-off California, heard him out, and decided that he was the kind of able student Annapolis needed. He appointed him to the Academy, from which Michelson graduated four years later.

During the next few years Michelson became an instructor in physics and chemistry at Annapolis, and found that he was fascinated by the phenomena of the speed of light. In 1878 he computed the speed of light to be 186,508 miles per second, a discovery that won for him instant acclaim and invitations to devote his time to research rather than to teaching.

After a few years attending lectures and seminars with the eminent physicists of Europe, Michelson returned to the United States and devoted himself to developing an instrument known as an interferometer, which could measure tiny distances more accurately than the strongest microscope. He was intrigued by the question of whether there was independent motion by the earth, and carried on his experiments at the Case School in Cleveland, where he discovered that there was no drift in the ether surrounding the earth as had generally been assumed to be the case. His discovery proved of inestimable value to the development of the science of optics and helped lay the groundwork for Einstein's subsequent experiments in relativity.

Astronomers began to use Michelson's interferometer to determine the size of stars. The first recorded measurement of a star utilizing Michelson's invention took place in 1920 at the famous Mount Wilson Observatory in California.

Another device that Michelson created was the echelon spectroscope, which enabled a viewer to see molecules in the act of vibration when a given substance was heated. Michelson was also anxious to determine the rigidity of the earth, and he developed a test involving the laying of long pipes half-filled with water at a depth of six feet underground and determining the strength of tidal pulls, the earth's size, and that of the sun and the moon, and proving that the interior of the earth was both strong as steel and simultaneously elastic.

Later he devised a method of utilizing the speed of light as a method for measuring the entire world. Michelson's pre-eminence as a scientist led to his election to the presidency of the American Association for the Advancement of Science and of the National Academy of Science. He was honored by many other scientific bodies around the world, and in 1907 received the highest award from the Royal Society of London—the oldest scientific body in history—which bestowed the Copley Medal on him.

In that same year, Michelson was awarded the Nobel Prize in physics, which was a great tribute not only to him but also to the United States since he became the first American ever to receive a Nobel Prize.

He died in Pasadena, California, in 1931, still

experimenting, still trying to unlock the earth's secrets for the benefit of mankind. Like Einstein, he loved to play the violin, and also enjoyed relaxing with a paintbrush and easel. His book *Light Waves and Their Uses* has been acclaimed a modern scientific classic.

Had an ambitious seventeen-year-old immigrant boy from California not pressed the President of the United States for an interview and won an appointment to Annapolis, who knows whether the world as we know it today would be quite the same?

JOSHUA LEDERBERG
The Extraordinary Bacteriologist

HE WAS BORN in Montclair, New Jersey, but was raised in the Washington Heights neighborhood of upper Manhattan, not far from Columbia University. His father was an Orthodox rabbi, and young Joshua received a traditional Jewish upbringing.

His early interest in the world of science led him to attend the Stuyvesant High School, where the natural sciences and mathematics are stressed. At the age of nineteen he graduated from Columbia, and soon enrolled in the medical school attached to the university.

Lederberg's probing mind came to the attention of one of the leading bacteriologists of the time, Edward L. Tatum, who invited him to come to Yale and help in research—specifically genetic research of bacteria.

It was a happy choice for both Lederberg and Tatum, and the young scientist soon found his life's work in microbiology research. After receiving his doctoral degree in microbiology from Yale, Lederberg went to the University of Wisconsin, where he set up a department of medical genetics. Later he became head of a similar department at Stanford University in California.

In 1958, at the age of thirty-three, Dr. Joshua Lederberg was awarded the Nobel Prize in physiology and medicine together with Dr. Tatum and Dr. George Beadle. The award was bestowed for the work the three had done in discovering that all biological reactions, including those in bacteria, are the result of genetic influence.

Working with powerful microscopes, the researchers found that even among the tiny cells of bacteria there is a system of genetic inheritance, just as there is in higher plant and animal life.

Subsequent studies conducted by Dr. Lederberg and others led to the discovery that where viruses invade bacteria, they often transmit additional characteristics, thus in effect leading to the development of a new strain of bacteria.

Although this may seem to be of marginal interest to the average person, it is of vital importance to cancer-research specialists since it means that a virus is capable of changing a normal cell into a malignant one.

Dr. Lederberg's pioneering work in the genetics

of bacteria has helped to open up a whole new area of study, which it is hoped may one day help to find a cure for the scourge of cancer.

Always anxious to have the general public made more cognizant of new medical and scientific developments, Dr. Lederberg for a number of years wrote a weekly newspaper column titled "Science and Man," which was widely syndicated.

He has also taken a strong, personal interest in the scientific achievements of Israel's universities and research centers, reflecting perhaps his own genetic background: Not only was his father a rabbi but his family's genealogy shows a long line of rabbis, many of whom lived in Palestine long before the establishment of modern Israel.

In recent years Dr. Lederberg has expanded his studies to include the chemical origin and evolution of life, space biology, and the social consequences of genetic changes in humans. From 1961 to 1978 he directed the Kennedy Laboratories for Molecular Biology and Medicine.

In 1978 he was elected president of Rockefeller University in New York, the crowning achievement of his distinguished career. When the announcement of Dr. Lederberg's elevation to that prestigious post was made, Rockefeller University said that he was one of the pioneers who has transformed the "genetics of micro-organisms into a comprehensive field of research" that is invaluable for biomedical research. The scientific community is hopeful that one of the youngest Nobel laureates will continue to make vital contributions to mankind's knowledge of itself.

MORDECAI ANILEWICZ
He Led the Warsaw Ghetto Uprising

VISITORS TO ISRAEL have heard of a kibbutz named Yad Mordecai, but not everyone knows that it was named for a twenty-four-year-old Polish Jew whose heroism has been compared to that of the ancient Maccabees.

Mordecai Anilewicz was born in Poland in 1919. In his youth he was attracted to the Zionist movement and dreamed of the day when he and his friends could settle in Israel and help build a Jewish homeland based on the principles of social and economic justice. Those who knew him as a student, when he was about eighteen or nineteen, described him as a soft-spoken, gentle, and scholarly person who always showed an intense interest in economics. He was convinced that if the world's economic structure could be turned around, if poor people would have more funds to improve their lives, the world would be a better and more peaceful place to live in.

On the morning of September 1, 1939, the world awoke to learn that the Germans had launched a massive attack on Poland, which was the beginning of World War II. Mordecai tried to escape across the Polish-Rumanian border, hoping to reach Palestine, but he and his friends were stopped at the border and sent back to Warsaw. The Germans very quickly succeeded in reducing Poland to a state of virtual enslavement and soon turned their attention to the Jews.

There were at the time more than three million Jews in Poland, one of the largest communities in the world. Large segments of the population were unable to believe that the Nazi announcements of "death to the Jews" were real, but within a relatively short time, hundreds of thousands of Jews had been imprisoned in walled-in ghettos, labor camps, and concentration camps. When the Russians seized part of the western sectors of Poland in advance of the German invaders, thousands of more fortunate Polish Jews were rescued.

When young Mordecai found himself in the Warsaw ghetto, together with scores of thousands of other Jews, he knew that he had to do everything he could to help the inmates of the huge prison survive. He organized a system of food and clothing rationing, and set up classes for the small children. In mid-1942, some two years after the Nazi conquest of Poland, he and other Warsaw ghetto leaders learned what was happening to the Jews of Poland under the new German regime— they were being systematically murdered.

Plans were made to organize some kind of resistance movement, despite the obviously difficult obstacles. Anilewicz was named commander of the new, secret Jewish Fighting Organization, which was made up of people who were determined to fight back if the Germans tried to ship the Jews to death camps, as they knew they would.

Obtaining arms was a major problem, with some members of the Polish resistance movement willing to co-operate with the Jews but others utterly opposed. Gradually some arms were smuggled into the ghetto, and utmost secrecy had to be maintained about the whole operation since it was suspected, correctly, that there were informers among the ghetto inhabitants.

Mordecai Anilewicz, in his twenty-fourth year of life, in early 1943, had taken over the command of the resistance movement within the ghetto. He was no longer a studious type but a tough commander in a situation that called for resolute action. He and his fellow resistance leaders deeply regretted that they had waited some three years to organize their campaign of resistance to the Germans. They now knew that the only fate that awaited the vast majority of Jews in Poland and other parts of Europe under Nazi domination was deliberate annihilation, and they were determined to fight back and to take as many of the enemy with them as possible to their graves.

Young men and women were taught how to fight with homemade weapons, as well as with the pitifully small number of real guns that had managed to reach the Jews inside the ghetto. On April 18, 1943, the first night of Passover, the resistance fighters under Mordecai's command were on the alert. There were more Jews in the ghetto at that time than normally since a number of Warsaw Jews who had been living outside the walls had sneaked back in, in order to celebrate the Passover in a more Jewish environment.

Early in the morning of April 19 a heavily armed German force, including Latvian collaborators, invaded the ghetto and were met by a "hail of grenades, bottles, bombs, and rifle shots— and the only machine gun did not err," a report of the event noted, adding that the Nazis quickly withdrew from the ghetto area.

More military forces were thrown into the attack by the Germans, who also brought in artillery, which the Jews of course did not have. The battle raged for many hours, and at nightfall the Germans withdrew, giving the Jews a brief respite. At sundown some of the more observant Jews sat down to the traditional Passover Seder celebrations, which were conducted in bunkers.

The tempo of the fighting continued all through the balance of the month of April, and Jews and Germans lost their lives daily. On May 8, after weeks of fierce fighting, the Germans succeeded in learning the location of the command bunker from which Anilewicz and other leaders conducted the battles. To this day no one knows how they learned of the secret headquarters.

Surrounded by the Germans who had thrown gas into the bunker, the Jewish resistance leaders took their own lives rather than fall into the hands of the Nazis. One account says that Anilewicz committed suicide and another reports he died fighting. The German commandant of the battle against the ghetto regretted that he could not interrogate the leaders of the revolt, including Anilewicz.

The young Polish Jew was described by Emmanuel Ringleblum, who kept an invaluable diary of the events of the Warsaw Ghetto Uprising, as "one of the finest and noblest warriors, who from the beginning put his life at the service of his people."

The courage that Mordecai Anilewicz displayed served as a source of inspiration to other Jews caught in the Nazi trap, and later to the Israelis when they fought against invading Arab forces. A kibbutz in the northern part of the Negev in Israel, Yad Mordecai, was named for him—and, during the crucial battles between the beleaguered Israeli forces and the far larger Egyptian army attacking from the south in 1948 the kibbutz stood fast, preventing the planned assault on Tel Aviv.

A statue of Mordecai Anilewicz near the museum dedicated to the Warsaw Ghetto Uprising located in kibbutz Yad Mordecai shows him standing on the alert, grenade in hand, ready to resist any attack on his people.

Louis D. Brandeis
Supreme Court Justice

PRESIDENT FRANKLIN ROOSEVELT used to call him affectionately "Isaiah," and there was about him an aura of the ancient prophet. Many compared him—in manner, appearance, views—to Lincoln. As a young attorney in Boston, he came to be known as the "people's advocate" because he always seemed to be defending the rights of the poor, the downtrodden, and those who could never hope to approach high-priced lawyers for help.

Despite stiff opposition in the Senate, which debated the issue for four months, he became the first Jew to serve on the Supreme Court, a position he filled with distinction. Many believed that, had he not been Jewish, he would certainly have been named Chief Justice. He was without a doubt one of the great Jewish personalities produced in America.

He was born in 1856 and raised in Louisville, Kentucky, and as a small child remembered seeing his mother helping in the local canteen, providing food and drink to Union soldiers during the Civil War. His parents had been immigrants from Bohemia (part of Czechoslovakia today), and he grew up in a home where the needs of the impoverished and the ill-treatment of many social and economic groups were genuine sources of concern.

After graduating from a local high school at fifteen, Brandeis entered Harvard Law School and at the age of twenty became a lawyer. Together with a classmate, he started practicing in Boston, and by the end of a decade he had achieved a reputation as a clearheaded, courageous attorney who cared deeply about such issues as shortening workers' hours, child labor, and workmen's compensation. He and his wife, Alice, lived simple, frugal lives, and he was happy to be able to help those less fortunate than he.

He loved everything American, particularly after having spent a few years studying in a school in Germany. Although he admitted that the scholarly levels in Germany were high, he hated the disciplinary methods employed. "In Louisville," he once said, "you could whistle." He never denied that he was Jewish, nor did he ever personally feel any exposure to overt anti-Semitism. He contributed to local Jewish charities on a purely philanthropic basis, but until past the age of fifty he was isolated from the mainstream of the Jewish community.

All that changed in 1910, when he was asked to come down from Boston to New York and arbitrate a major clash in the garment industry between the employers and workers. For the first time in his life, he got to know East European Jews, most of whom spoke Yiddish, many of whom declared themselves to be Zionists, and most of whom he came to admire for their passionate interest in the welfare of their coreligionists.

He began to read Jewish history, and made inquiries about the then brand-new Zionist movement launched by Theodor Herzl at the first World Zionist Congress in Basel, Switzerland. An early Zionist leader, Jacob de Haas, who was the editor of a Jewish newspaper in Boston, helped influence Brandeis' thinking, too.

In the course of time, Brandeis announced that he was a Zionist, explaining, "My approach to Zionism was through Americanism. In time, practical experience and observation convinced me that Jews were by reason of their traditions and their character peculiarly fitted for the attainment of American ideals. Gradually it became clear to me that to be good Americans we must be better Jews, and to be better Jews we must become Zionists. Jewish life cannot be preserved and developed, assimilation cannot be averted, unless

53

there be established in the fatherland a center from which the Jewish spirit may radiate and give to the Jews scattered throughout the world that inspiration which springs from the memories of a great past and the hope of a great future."

When World War I broke out, he became head of the Zionist movement in the United States. He was a close friend of President Woodrow Wilson and high American officials, and is credited with securing support for the Balfour Declaration and for the British Mandate over a territory with adequate boundaries.

Despite his judicial bearing, he was essentially a man of action and of logic. In 1915, while the war raged in Europe, a threat of famine hung over the people of Asia Minor. He organized a nationwide campaign, appealing to all people to help stave off a disaster. By March, two months after the drive had been announced, a mercy ship filled with nine hundred tons of food sailed for Jaffa from Philadelphia, preventing a great loss of life.

As the war drew to an end and the defeat of Germany was in sight, Brandeis addressed a large Zionist meeting, urging his audience to look ahead to the peace. "By battling for the Zionist cause," he declared, "the American ideal of democracy, of social justice, and of liberty will be given wider expression. By concrete action, the prayer of twenty centuries will be made to come true."

He visited Palestine soon after the war ended

and came away with mixed feelings: The spirit of the idealistic pioneers exhilarated him, but the sight of the disease-ridden malaria swamps filled him with sorrow. He returned to the United States more determined than ever to turn the Zionist movement into an instrumentality of practical support for the early pioneering efforts, and stressed the need for modern capital investments in industry as well as in agriculture.

As a justice of the Supreme Court, he gave enormous prestige to the Zionist movement in the United States and did not hesitate to debate the wealthier elements of the community who feared that their overt support for creating a Jewish homeland would subject them to criticism from non-Jewish Americans.

He asserted, "I have been to a great extent separated from Jews. I am very ignorant in things Jewish. But recent experiences, public and professional, have taught me this: I find Jews possessed of those very qualities which we of the twentieth century seek to develop in our struggle for justice and democracy, a deep moral feeling which makes them capable of noble acts, a deep sense of the brotherhood of man, and a high intelligence, the fruit of three thousand years of civilization.

"These experiences have made me feel that the Jewish people have something which should be saved for the world, that the Jewish people should be preserved, and that it is our duty to pursue that method of saving which most promises success."

On the bench, Brandeis became famous as a moralist and teacher. Even during periods in American history when members of Congress were working to defeat new social legislation, he and his close friend and colleague, Chief Justice Oliver Wendell Holmes, explained that the U. S. Constitution was not restricted to a single economic credo and that therefore prevention of progressive social legislation was contrary to the spirit of the Founding Fathers.

His judicial decisions not only backed such measures as minimum wage laws, price controls, and protection of labor unions against injunctions but also emphasized the need for sharing power between the federal government and the individual states in the Union.

At the age of eighty-five, Brandeis retired from the Supreme Court, having left an indelible mark on American history. In Israel a kibbutz, Ein Hashofet ("Spring of the Judge"), was named for him, and in Waltham, Massachusetts, not far from Boston, where he began his career, a Jewish-sponsored university bears his name.

LENA KUCHLER
"Mother" of a Hundred Children

THERE WAS A WOMAN living in Israel who was looked upon as the mother of some one hundred children—and the grandmother of many more scores of young Israeli children. Indeed, she also had "children" and "grandchildren" in the United States and in other parts of the world.

And yet, in point of fact, this remarkable woman was the mother of only one lovely young lady, Shira. The woman's name was Lena Kuchler, and in the annals of the Jewish people she will always be remembered as a true heroine of an era that was marked by unparalleled brutality.

The story begins at the time of the outbreak of World War II, in 1939. Lena Kuchler was a young Jewish wife and mother when Hitler's army invaded Poland, where she and her family lived. She was an educator, specializing in child psychology.

The panic that followed on the heels of the German invasion, the roundups of Jews and their imprisonment in camps and ghettos, the attempts to hide from the ruthless enemy, the systematic massacres—all these have been well chronicled. It was a disastrous time for all people in Poland, but for the Polish Jews it was a time of utmost peril: The Nazis were bent on carrying out their threat of extinction of all Jews in Europe.

Lena and her family sought refuge in a small village, most of whose residents were not Jewish. At one point she left her small child with a Gentile family for safekeeping; her husband decided to try to evade the Nazis by hiding out in the woods, and she herself opted to live as a Christian maid. Her blond hair and Slavic appearance led her to believe that this was the best way to outsmart the Germans.

She found employment with a family living in a distant rural area, where she came to be regarded as a Christian Polish woman who did her job well.

This was how she spent the early years of the war, afraid to breathe the truth about her identity, constantly worried about her small child, wondering about the fate of her husband, her family, her friends. Although she was in an isolated community, she nevertheless began to hear of the unceasing massacre of Jews throughout Nazi-occupied territories, including Poland. She found herself living as though in suspended animation. She waited for the nightmare to come to an end.

Alone, at night, she would lie on her cot, tears filling her eyes, wondering, worrying, knowing that she could do nothing except what she was doing—remaining in hiding from the angel of death who wore a swastika on his uniform.

The days stretched into months, the months into years—and then, one day, from the west, Russian troops began to overrun the farm where she had been living in limbo, a self-imprisoned survivor, and at last she was free to look for her family.

With incredible difficulties she made her way back home, while all around her the fighting continued, although gradually it became clear that it was only a matter of time before the Nazi war machine was destroyed and the Nazi reign of evil and terror came to an end.

She returned home and found devastation. Her parents, her husband, her child—all had "disappeared" in the giant graveyard the Nazis had dug in the territory they seized. She was thrown into deep shock—physical, mental, emotional. Lena became a broken person, hating herself for having survived while virtually everyone else had perished.

But there were some other survivors after all, the so-called *shearith hapleitah*. Children of varying ages, who had been kept hidden and alive in monasteries and convents by kindly priests and nuns, now emerged from their hiding places, proclaiming in their own way that they were Jews. Other children, who had been hidden on remote farms by peasants who had hoped to be rewarded handsomely for their lifesaving, now found themselves thrown out once it became known that the parents—and the parents' funds—would never be seen again.

These sick, emaciated, destitute children were brought together in a Jewish communal residence, and an effort was made to heal them. Funds and supplies were made available by a number of Jewish relief organizations, but the situation was desperate and called for much more than money.

The surviving children had ceased being children. They did not sing or laugh or play. They looked forlorn, abandoned, hopeless. Many were ill, suffering from a wide variety of diseases. All of them were undernourished. Some of the older ones had taken to stealing, and felt no compunctions about doing so.

It was around this time that the local aid organization discovered Lena. She was, after all, a child psychologist and an educator. She knew about children. She had suffered too. The group's leaders persuaded her to try to help the children in any and every way she could.

Reluctant at first, she slowly overcame her inner sense of hopelessness and bitterness and began to work, trying to rebuild the lives of the children put in her care. Instinctively she knew that if she could help them, she would be rebuilding her own life, too.

She organized classes, recruited medical help,

found a clean mountain-resort residence in the Zakopane area where the children could breathe fresh air and eat nourishing food, and where—she hoped—they could begin to learn, and to sing, to play, to hope.

By 1946 nearly a year after the war ended, the miracle had begun to work: Some one hundred children in her care were living in Zakopane, and each day saw them gaining daily, in their health, in their minds, in their spirits.

And then one day the little private world they had created in the Zakopane mountain resort was shattered when news arrived of an outbreak of a postwar series of pogroms against the surviving Jews in Poland. This was still two years before there was an Israel, but Lena decided that the best hope for her children was to get them, somehow, to Palestine.

A few weeks after the first pogroms erupted in Poland, the children's residence in Zakopane was attacked, with Lena and a number of the older children defending themselves and the younger children until help arrived.

Soon after, without requisite official documents, Lena led her children, stealthily and unofficially, across the border into Czechoslovakia, and eventually to southern France, from where shiploads of Jews were being smuggled to Palestine despite the ban on any new Jewish immigration imposed by the British Mandatory power.

Eventually, Lena led her family of one hundred

children to Palestine, shortly before the Jewish community there established the State of Israel. The vast majority of the children have grown up in Israel, have found jobs, married, and look upon Lena Kuchler as their mother—and their children regard her as their grandmother.

Lena remarried in Israel, where she gave birth to a daughter. She worked in her profession of child psychology, seeking to help children who needed guidance and support. Nearly every day the mail brought news from her children, none of whom could ever forget that she led them across the threshold of despair to hope and a new life.

She died in Israel in 1987.

GERARD SWOPE
For Israel's Future Engineers

NOWADAYS THERE ARE Jewish engineers galore. Jewish young men and women interested in entering virtually any branch of the vast world of engineering know that the doors of MIT, Cal Tech, and scores of other important educational institutions specializing in the engineering sciences are wide open to them, and admittance is based on ability and academic standing.

But this was not always so. Eighty or ninety years ago (and until even more recently than that), the field of engineering did not take kindly to Jewish applicants. Some students, like their colleagues in medicine, went abroad to study; some fought valiantly to be admitted, and eventually won their battle; some changed their names in the hope that their Jewish origins would escape notice; and some went to the Hebrew Technical Institute in New York, which flourished for a period, and is still active in providing scholarships for needy students.

One of these would-be engineers was a brilliant young man born in Missouri in 1872, the grandson of a rabbi. The boy's name was Gershon Schwab. There was no doubt in his mind what he wanted to do with his life—engineering, especially the growing new field of electrical engineering, was his passion, and he was determined to attain his maximum potential.

He left his home and went east, to Cambridge, Massachusetts, the home of MIT and Harvard. In the course of the move, he altered his name, and his MIT application was approved. The student from Missouri known now as Gerard Swope turned in first rate work, and when he graduated from MIT as an engineer, it was with top honors. A brilliant future was predicted for him.

He found a job in a small company, and very soon began to rise to ever-increasing levels of responsibility. The fact that he was a Jew had been all but erased from his mind. He concentrated on building his promising career. The young engineer's talents as an administrator were soon revealed, as was his ability to speak before audiences of investors and businessmen.

One day he found himself in a courtroom defending his company in an industrial dispute, arguing his case against the giant General Electric firm. When the trial was over and GE had lost, a strange thing happened—the General Electric people offered the young engineering executive a bigger job than he held at the time in his own firm. He decided to accept.

He rose quickly in the ranks of General Electric, and in the course of time became its president and chief executive officer, a position he was to retain for many years, leading the company upward and onward in the expanding fields of energy, and machinery and appliances based on electrical power. The young man, born Gershon Schwab but now known only as Gerard Swope, had certainly made it big. For all intents and purposes, he lived the life of a non-Jew.

He married a Gentile woman. Children were born and reared; everything was fine and everyone was happy. But there is an old saying that truth is stranger than fiction: Who could really know what went on in the heart and mind of this major American industrial executive?

One wonders how this grandson of a rabbi reacted to scenes of Yiddish-speaking Jewish refugees fleeing from eastern Europe, trying to make a new life for themselves in America. How did he feel when he picked up his newspaper in November 1917 and read that the British government had proclaimed its readiness to support the establishment of a Jewish homeland in Palestine? And in the early 1930s, when the scourge of

Nazism threatened to take over all of civilization, how did he respond to scenes of his fellow Jews being driven into concentration camps or locked up in ghettos? We shall never know precisely, because he is dead now, but something must have stirred within him; somehow the tiny spark of his Jewishness must have remained alive, even though practically no one knew that this powerful figure in American economic life was himself a Jew.

And then on impulse he went one evening to hear a talk by a New York lawyer, Abraham Tulin, a lifelong Zionist, on the geopolitical possibilities that confronted the world after the end of World War II. The speaker wove into his talk the hopes that then existed for the new, barely two-year-old State of Israel. Something in that talk fanned that tiny spark of Jewishness in the executive's heart, making it glow just a little brighter.

He invited Tulin to lunch; they talked at length and became friends. The president of General Electric then told his new friend what almost no one knew—that he was himself a Jew. Now in his late seventies, with his children grown and on their own, he felt he would like to "do something" for the people he belonged to and from whom he had estranged himself for most of his life.

The attorney was an active leader of a small American group that was providing support for a small, still struggling engineering school in Israel, the Technion-Israel Institute of Technology in

Haifa. Cautiously, he suggested that his particular institution was perhaps a vehicle through which Swope could provide greatly needed help to Israel, which was in urgent need of a steady stream of modern, well-trained engineers.

The idea appealed to Swope, and soon wheels began to turn. He paid a visit to Israel in the early years when food rationing was in force, new immigrants were still living in tents, and the chief assets of the country were hope and courage. He visited the small campus of the Technion and was shown land that had been set aside for construction of a new network of classrooms, laboratories, workshops, libraries, and dormitories for a vastly enlarged campus. He met with David Ben-Gurion, the Prime Minister, and talked with fellow engineers, students, and Technion faculty members.

He toured the country, seeing with his own eyes places that he dimly remembered hearing about in his early youth—Jerusalem, Beersheba, Galilee, Ashkelon. He spent time visiting the new immigrants, among them survivors of the concentration camps, whose arms remained tattooed with the numbers burned into their flesh by the Nazis.

He returned to the United States, his mind made up about what he was going to do. He told his lawyer friend that he did not want to have any buildings named for him; he wanted instead to help students acquire an engineering education. He had become a very rich man, and he had decided to provide amply for his children (his wife had died) and then to leave the remainder of his estate to the Technion to become a perpetual source of aid to needy students and to attract the very best faculty members possible.

There was no lack of complicated legal tax problems in the decision, but these were overcome under Tulin's guidance as a legal adviser. Eventually a fund of more than eight million dollars was established, which became the basis of the Technion's scholarship fund. It is now valued at many millions of dollars, and has already provided help for many hundreds of students.

There is no doubt that in the course of time thousands of students in future generations will be aided to obtain an engineering education at the Technion because a stilled Jewish voice cried out in the heart of one man.

HERMAN WOUK
Literary Luminary

THE NAME OF HERMAN WOUK is known and admired in every part of the world. His books have been translated into numerous languages, and he was awarded the Pulitzer Prize for his memorable novel of World War II, *The Caine Mutiny*.

He is not only an observant Jew but one who has returned to a traditional Jewish way of life after having been exposed to a secular, irreligious environment in his college years and while he was active as an advertising and radio writer. He has been a visiting professor of English at Yeshiva University and has actively supported synagogues and educational institutions both in the United States and Israel.

In addition to his best-selling novels, he has written a book titled *This Is My God*, in which he undertakes to explain his own faith in the Jewish way of life—a book that has remained in print for nearly a generation and that has undoubtedly influenced Jewish men and women to take a new look at their religious heritage.

Wouk was born in New York in 1915. He was a successful radio writer for some six years before entering the Navy in World War II. He served in the Pacific for four years, an experience that he used to produce *The Caine Mutiny*. Among his other books are *Marjorie Morningstar*, *Youngblood Hawke*, *The Winds of War*, and *War and Remembrance*.

He has declared himself to be a religious Jew, aware of the fact that his vast reputation as a novelist may influence some members of the current and newer generation of Jews, especially in the United States. In *This Is My God* he wrote:

> Judaism is part of my life and of my family's life. . . . Religious people tend to encounter, among those who are not, a cemented certainty that belief in God is a crutch for the weak and the fearful. It would be just as silly to assert that disbelief in God is a crutch for the immoral and the ill-read. . . . I believe the survival of the Jewish people looks like the hand of Providence in history, and I also believe in the law of Moses as the key to our survival. . . . I believe it is our lot to live and serve in our old identity, until the promised

day when the Lord will be one and his name one in all the earth. I think the extinction of Jewish learning and Jewish faith would be a measureless tragedy.

Wouk has established at the religiously oriented Bar-Ilan University in Israel a student scholarship in memory of his grandfather, Rabbi Mendel Leib Levine, whom he has described as follows:

His lifetime of ninety-four years stretched from the last days of Abraham Lincoln to the first years of the nuclear era. He served as a Jewish jurist and minister under czarism and communism, in the freedom of America, and in the reborn land of Israel, where his bones lie.

Compared with other well-known authors, Wouk is a relatively private person. He is a daily worshiper at an Orthodox synagogue in Washington, where he lives, and devotes time each day to the study of the Talmud. He does not enjoy the lecture circuit and does not usually like to address large gatherings, even if they are for worthy causes which he fully supports.

On the rare occasions when he consents to speak to a Jewish fund-raising meeting, the only condition that he stipulates is that the food served be strictly kosher. At the time of their marriage, his wife was a Gentile, but she has since become a convert to Judaism and shares her husband's strong convictions about traditional Judaism.

ISRAEL BAAL
SHEM TOV
Master of the Good Name

HE WAS BORN IN 1700 in a small *shtetl* in Poland, the kind of community in which very small boys, sometimes no older than five or six, could be seen at the break of dawn rushing off to their daily religious-school classes. When he was himself no more than about twelve, and an orphan who was cared for by the community as a whole, Israel ben Eliezer—who many years later was to become known as Israel Baal Shem Tov—used to escort the young boys to class every morning (except, of course, on the Sabbath, when everyone went to services in the synagogue).

People in the town noticed something different as soon as the young man became the official escort of the young students. The boys, even at an

73

early hour, before they had had much more than a morsel of bread and a few swallows of tea, would march down the unpaved road to school singing, smiling, laughing as though they were going to a party. It seems that young Israel had begun to teach the students that everything around them—the rising sun in the early hours of the day, the singing of birds along the way, the smell of fresh-cut hay in the nearby fields, indeed everything in the world—was beautiful, God-given, and deserved to be greeted with joy and song. This is how he had begun to understand the world around him, and he began to explain his ideas to the boys in his care— and apparently they liked what they heard and preferred to sing and smile rather than proceed to school in a somber, serious manner as they had been taught to do previously.

This philosophy that the young man developed remained with him all his life, and in the course of time he became the founder of a Jewish religious movement which stressed that the blessings of the world around us should be seen and appreciated, and admired in song. The movement eventually became known as the Hasidic movement, and those who belonged were known as Hasidim, or "Pious Ones." There are today followers of the Hasidic philosophy in all parts of the world, who have shown that song and dance can make people as appreciative of Judaism as a lifetime of study. The Hasidim do not believe in fancy clothes or expensive homes or cars, but rather that every

Jewish family should have the minimum needed for a decent standard of life, and should devote some time to study and much time to joyous song, prayer, and enjoyment of life. Of course, they also stress the importance of observing each and every commandment of Jewish religious life, and have even added a few customs and practices of their own.

When he was about eighteen, Israel ben Eliezer was given the job of *shamash* or sexton of the local synagogue. His job was to take care of the books used for study and worship, to call people to the various sections of the reading of the Torah, and to welcome strangers who would drop in and find a resting place in the synagogue for the night.

He was not a scholar by nature, and some people also said he was "strange," for he never tired of talking of the beauty and wonder of nature and of the foolishness of trying to make money so as to have a bigger house or a newer carriage. A few years passed, and he tired of his job as a shamash and began to wander around the countryside, sleeping in various synagogues, dressed as a woodcutter, and making friends of the Christian peasants whom he met and with whom he sometimes camped.

Eventually he married the daughter of a respected rabbi, even though he himself was not a learned man and it was against tradition for a rabbi's daughter to marry someone who was relatively uneducated. But there was something in the eyes of the young man that attracted the girl's father when he first met Israel, and Hannah, the bride-to-be, agreed to her father's wish that they marry. Deep in her heart she believed that her husband, despite his rough clothing and simple ways, must really be a righteous, saintly person.

For a few years the young couple lived in a poor hut in the mountains, hardly able to scrape out a living. Later, Hannah's brother, Rabbi Gershon, bought an inn for the young couple so they they could live more comfortably. Both Israel and Hannah were well suited to their new business, making the guests who stayed with them as comfortable and welcome as possible. Most of the work, however, fell on Hannah's shoulders, because her husband often spent long hours in the nearby woods, deep in thought, and sometimes praying alone in the fields for hours at a time.

There was one thing that people began to discover in Israel—a sympathetic listener. They came to him from the nearby countryside, explaining their troubles and problems, asking for his advice and guidance. everyone seemed to find in him a source of wisdom and comfort, and his own strong faith in God helped many people overcome their own personal and family troubles.

Gradually he came to be known as Israel Baal Shem Tov, or "Israel, the Master of the Good Name." He began to visit nearby communities, to encourage Jews who were downhearted, to assure them that they were all holy and loved in the eyes of God, and so long as they lived as good, God-fearing people, all would be well. Soon the reputation of the Baal Shem Tov spread far and wide, and before long those who agreed with his views had organized the Hasidic movement.

Although there were many Jews who disapproved of the group's emphasis on joy in study and prayer, the movement grew very quickly. Visiting a service of the Hasidim meant seeing men and women profoundly immersed in prayer, singing and swaying with a sense of closeness to God that was quite different from the more formal services of most other Jews. The Hasidim looked upon the Baal Shem Tov as a rebbe, a truly righteous leader whose personal example inspired them to seek to lead lives of simplicity and afforded them an opportunity to become more and more in tune with the spirit of the Torah.

Israel Baal Shem Tov never wrote any books, but everything he ever said was remembered and repeated, so that every Hasid after a while could cite his words of wisdom as a source of guidance.

When the Baal Shem Tov died in 1760, he left behind him a movement of tens of thousands of Hasidic followers, and soon there grew up other Rebbes who preached the importance of personal commitment to God and who denied that intense study was the only way for Jews to attain the highest rung on the ladder that would lead to a fully rewarding life.

One of the leading Hasidic leaders in the world

today is the Lubavitcher Rebbe, whose headquarters are in Brooklyn, New York. There are several hundred thousand Jews who are known as Lubavitch Hasidim scattered throughout the world, and although they now encourage study to a far greater degree than did the early followers of the Baal Shem Tov, the basic philosophy of the group has not changed. That is why a visit to a Hasidic synagogue or to a *farbrengung*, a kind of lecture on the Torah accompanied by much singing, is a very special experience.

The followers of the Hasidic movement managed, during more than sixty years of the Soviet Union's determined campaign to wipe out all forms of religion, to continue to live as observant Jews, although they had to do so in complete secrecy. Several thousand of these Soviet Hasidim have managed to reach Israel and the United States, where they now follow their traditional way of life without fear of interference.

One of the frequently quoted phrases of Israel Baal Shem Tov is, "Whoever lives in joy does his Creator's will. It is the goal of my whole life on earth to show my brethren, by living example, how one may serve God with merriment and rejoicing. He who is full of joy is full of love for his fellow men and all fellow creatures."

HERMAN BRANOVER
Physicist with a Yarmulke

ONE OF THE WORLD'S largest Jewish communities has always been that of Russia. Before the outbreak of the First World War, when Jews in Russia lived under a crucl and hated czarist regime, hundreds of thousands made their way out of the country, most of them finding new homes and new lives in the United States and South America, and a smaller number in Palestine, then beginning to develop as an embryonic Jewish homeland.

Toward the end of World War I, in 1917, revolution erupted in Russia and the czarist regime was overthrown, replaced by a Communist government that preached full equality. Another strong principle that guided the new Soviet authorities was total opposition to religion, including of course Judaism. For more than sixty years the Jewish population of Russia has been denied an opportunity to practice the basic tenets of the ancient Jewish faith. Owning a copy of the Bible became a punishable offense. Any interest in the Zionist movement or in the Hebrew language was strictly forbidden. The prospects for the continuation of the Jewish community as a religious or cultural entity in the Soviet Union looked very dim. Soviet Jews were not permitted to maintain any ties with organized Jewish groups abroad, and even individual correspondence between Russian Jews and relatives abroad was frowned upon.

Hundreds of thousands of Russian Jews were massacred by the Nazis when they invaded the Soviet Union in the summer of 1941. When the war ended, there were estimated to be some three million Jews in Russia, saved from the Nazis but gradually beginning to be totally assimilated, their religious and cultural heritage fading with each passing day.

There were a few notable exceptions to the general rule. The Hasidic movement, which had had large numbers of followers in Russia, struggled to keep up a semblance of religious life. Everything had to be carried out in total secrecy; anyone caught observing the Jewish holidays or studying a Jewish religious work could be arrested and shipped off to a Siberian labor camp. At the same time, the deeply rooted anti-Semitism that had existed from czarist days was still far from dormant. Despite the new Soviet laws proclaiming liberty and equality, Jews were often singled out for harassment and persecution.

The news of the establishment of Israel in 1948 kindled a spark among many Jews in the Soviet Union. Notwithstanding the fact that they had been cut off from the mainstream of Jewish life for many years, many Soviet Jews began to take heart that a Jewish state had been created and that Jews could live as Jews freely and openly there, as well as in other democratic countries. One such Jew who was deeply moved by the events around him was a physicist who had achieved a lofty reputation—Dr. Herman Branover, attached to the Academy of Science in Riga.

Born in Riga in 1931, he grew up in a nonreligious home that nevertheless had strong, positive feelings about Jewish culture. At the age of twenty-one he was studying in Leningrad and saw the Soviet authorities relegate more than twenty thousand books on Judaism to a public fire. It was a traumatic event for him. Secretly, he began to study Jewish history, religion, and philosophy. Five years later, at the age of twenty-six, knowing that he was taking a very dangerous step, he committed himself to leading the life of an observant, traditional Jew. He attached himself to the Hasidic movement in Riga and became one of them.

All this time he continued to pursue his scientific career, specializing in the field of magnetohydrodynamics. He wrote more than one hundred scientific papers in the field, about a third of which were translated into English and other languages, establishing his reputation as a world authority in this highly specialized field. At the same time, he translated the entire *Kitzur Shulhan Aruch*, the abbreviated code of Jewish laws, into Russian. His fellow Hasidim called him Rabbi, and indeed he was duly ordained after he was tested by overseas phone calls from leading rabbis in Israel and England.

In 1972 he embarked on a daring course: He began to teach Bible to young Jewish students, shrugging off the warnings from the authorities that he would be imprisoned if he persisted. Soon thereafter he applied for permission to emigrate to Israel, and it was only after the intervention of top world scientists, as well as leading American officials, that he and his family were allowed to leave.

Professor Branover today teaches physics at both the Tel Aviv and Ben-Gurion universities in Israel. He has formed an organization of Soviet Jewish academicians now living in Israel, seeking to teach them the basic tenets of Jewish religious life. He is also active in widespread educational programs in Israel aimed at bridging the information gap among the Russian immigrants who had been cut off from Judaism for more than half a century.

Professor Branover, who believes that "science helped me find my religious faith," has written, "Knowledge means setting up a world view that is free of contradictions, understanding the goodness of the world, and recognition of God. One must possess, in addition to intellect, logic and imagination . . . the ancient but still ringing words of the Torah express a wisdom that every man must strive to acquire for himself."

ALBERT EINSTEIN
Science with True Freedom

ALBERT EINSTEIN is universally acclaimed as one of the greatest scientists who ever lived. Although he is credited with having helped immeasurably to open up the era of the nuclear age, he was unalterably opposed to war and violence throughout his lifetime, and until his death he continued to urge that the atomic bomb be outlawed.

He was born in Ulm, Germany, in 1879, grew up in Munich, lived for a while in Italy with his parents, settled for a number of years in Switzerland, and then, as the wave of Nazism began to rise, left for the United States, where he lived in Princeton, New Jersey, carrying on his research at the Institute for Advanced Studies. He died in 1955, gratified that the dark forces of Hitlerism had been defeated, happy that Israel had been created, and fearful of the misuse of the atomic energy he had helped to unlock.

When he was a young student, some of his teachers thought he was backward, for he hated the regimented system of the German school, much preferring to stare into space and wonder about the world about him or to read poetry, philosophy, and books on mathematics. Games with toy soldiers, which were very popular at the time in Germany, more than bored him—they annoyed him. He explained once that he felt sorry for the soldiers because they had to do what they were told. This abiding passion for freedom remained with him always.

For a while his father worried that the boy was mentally deficient. One day he bought him a pocket compass and a book on geometry, and these small gifts were all that were needed to demonstrate once and for all that Albert was far from mentally weak. He developed an early interest in physics and began to devour everything he could find on the subject, reading books that were meant for specialists and seeming to understand them.

At twenty-one he graduated from the prestigious Zurich Polytechnic Institute, took a job in the Swiss patent office to provide for his needs, and began to concentrate on his research work. In 1905 he published a scientific paper on relativity, and in 1921 he was awarded the Nobel Prize in physics for his work. He had by then already achieved worldwide fame as a scientist and had been honored by many countries, including Germany, where a special research institution was set up so that he could devote full time to his work there—but his deep interest in peace and in Jewish affairs did not slacken.

At the invitation of Dr. Chaim Weizmann, the world Zionist leader, Einstein went to the United States in 1921 on a fund-raising visit in behalf of the nascent Jewish state. Later he spent two years as a visiting professor at the California Institute of Technology. He paid a visit to Palestine in the 1920s, meeting with scientists at the Hebrew University in Jerusalem and at the Technion-Israel Institute of Technology in Haifa, expressing the hope that important scientific developments would be forthcoming from those institutions. A tree he planted on the Technion campus is known to this day as the Einstein tree.

Although he was not a formally religious man, he used to say, when asked, that he believed in a "Supreme Intelligence" and that he had the feeling, as he carried out his experiments, that God "does not play dice with the world." In his home he always featured a menorah, the candelabrum that is symbolic of Judaism and that has become the official emblem of Israel.

One of the great moments of his life, he wrote, came when the State of Israel, after the death of its first president, Chaim Weizmann, invited him to become its second president. He declined because he did not feel he was qualified for the role but said the invitation had touched him deeply. Whenever he could, he urged support for Jewish education for the young, and for financial contributions to Israel. Himself a refugee from Nazi Germany, he could never forget the specter of armed Nazis roaming the streets of Germany, harassing and imprisoning Jews.

The world of science acknowledged that his work did more to revolutionize scientific thinking than that of any other single man. Numerous inventions and practical applications based on his theories and experiments led to television and sound motion pictures. None of these useful inventions really interested him, since he was concerned with the basic laws of the universe—time and space, mass and energy, gravity and space and time. He did not believe that the world had developed by happenstance and said instead that because of human inadequacy man has simply not yet learned to understand the fundamental law of nature.

In 1939 the Nazis launched World War II, and although Einstein was a confirmed pacifist, he concluded that the defeat of the Third Reich and its allies was more important than his espousing of pacifist philosophies. With the war raging in Europe and one European nation after another falling to the seemingly invincible Nazi armies, Einstein wrote a letter to President Franklin D. Roosevelt, saying in effect that it was now possible to release atomic energy—a possibility he dreaded, but he felt it was far more important for the United States to construct an atomic bomb before the Germans did.

Einstein's letter was the catalyst that helped initiate the secret American program to develop atomic bombs and usher in an era of nuclear power. Sending the letter had been a matter of profound inner turmoil for him: At the age of twenty-six he had announced the equation of mass with energy, and now, at sixty, he realized that his recommendation to the President of the United States could lead to a weapon that could imperil the future existence of mankind.

Despite all the honors that were thrust at him, he remained a humble and unassuming man all his life. He enjoyed a simple walk in Princeton, where he would chat idly with neighborhood youngsters. The money he received for the Nobel Prize was donated to charity. A story is told that a check for $1,500 sent him by a research foundation served for months as a bookmark—until he lost both the book and the bookmark.

He found great enjoyment in playing the violin and listening to music. Just prior to his death he was invited to attend a fund-raising dinner arranged by Yeshiva University in New York to help launch the projected Albert Einstein College of Medicine affiliated with the university. Surprising everyone, since he studiously avoided all public functions, he came to the dinner, as a result of which many millions of dollars were raised and the new medical school got off to a flying start.

His melancholy, philosophical face has appeared on the postage stamps of several countries, and the number of books and pamphlets written about him and his work is legion. Jewish schools, hospitals and other institutions bear his name.

He was deeply concerned for the survival and well-being of the new State of Israel, and agreed to go on a nationwide radio and television program in 1955—scheduled to coincide with Israel's seventh anniversary—to express his support for the Jewish state. But he became ill a few days before the program and died soon after.

He once said in a speech, "If we are to resist the powers that threaten intellectual and individual freedom, we must be very conscious of the fact that freedom itself is at stake—we must realize how much we owe to that freedom which our forefathers won through bitter struggle." That was in 1933, the year Hitler seized power in Germany.

Chances are that, if Einstein were alive today, he would voice the very same sentiments. Scientific progress without true freedom seemed meaningless to him.

CHAIM NACHMAN BIALIK
Poet Laureate of Israel

HE IS CONSIDERED the greatest poet of the Hebrew language in modern times. His poems have been set to music and sung by young and old. Students have memorized them and retained them throughout their lifetimes. He wrote of nature, of love, of sadness and joy, of the troubles of the Jewish people, of poverty, and of the rebirth of Israel.

Even among those who knew no Hebrew, Bialik came to be known as the modern poetic spokesman for the Jewish people, who expressed his people's great sorrows and at the same time offered them hope for a better tomorrow. His poems touched a special response in the hearts of Jewish men, women, and children, and he was acclaimed the poet laureate of the Jewish people of the twentieth century.

Bialik was born in a small village in czarist Russia in 1873. His father, a scholar who struggled to earn a living, died when Chaim was seven, and the young boy was sent to live with his grandfather, where he began to pursue the study of Talmud. The study of the Jewish Law did not satisfy him, however, and secretly he began to read Russian literature (an activity sharply condemned at the time by most traditional Jews).

As he grew up, he learned that other Jews in other parts of the world were planning to resettle the ancient Jewish homeland in Palestine and were reviving the use of Hebrew as a spoken and daily language. Still in his teens, he journeyed to the city of Odessa, on the Black Sea, then a principal center of Zionist activity. He had in the meantime written a poem, *El Hatzipor*—"To the Bird"— which he kept on a crumpled piece of paper in his pocket for months, too shy to share it with anyone.

With the help of a rabbi, his friend's father, he was introduced to Ahad Ha'am, the leading Zionist writer and editor of the day, who realized—after hearing Bialik's first poetic effort—that the shy young man was a natural writer and poet, and encouraged and helped him. Bialik's poem was published in a Hebrew magazine and this gave him the encouragement he needed to start producing many more poems. To support himself, he gave private lessons. Soon he met a local girl, fell in love, and was married.

Bialik was obsessed by the beauty of nature, and many of his poems were tributes to the simple joys of the outdoors. For a time he worked in his father-in-law's lumber business and used the long stretches of time he spent alone in the woods to read widely and to write.

When Theodor Herzl convened the first World Zionist Congress in Switzerland, Bialik greeted the event with a new poem. A few years later, when violent waves of pogroms broke out in Russia, he sat down and wrote bitterly of the slaughter and massacre. His words became an echo of what so many thousands of Jews in all parts of the world were feeling but could not articulate—and they were deeply grateful that Bialik could say it for them.

The spark of prophetic indignation burned in Bialik too, and when he felt that his people were not doing enough to defend and help their coreligionists who were being killed and oppressed, he spoke up sharply and clearly—in poetry. Gradually he became the voice of the Jewish people.

He began to embark on a career as a publisher, concentrating on the production of modern textbooks to teach Hebrew that incorporated the latest innovations in teaching methods. He was a rather poor businessman, but somehow he continued in his profession, preferring to live in the world of words and ideas rather than in any other world. Although as a younger man he had at one time thought of enrolling in a modern rabbinical seminary in Berlin, he abandoned the idea in favor of writing and publishing.

In 1917 Russia became the battleground for a revolution that saw the overthrow of the hated czarist regime and the installation of the new Communist government. One of the first steps taken by the new government, which was violently antireligious, was to outlaw the teaching of Hebrew, which was regarded as a language of the decadent Bible. Bialik and his fellow Hebrew writers, many of whom were concentrated in the Odessa area, realized that they could no longer remain in Russia. Through the intercession of the famous author Maxim Gorki, Bialik and his wife received permission to emigrate from Russia, and in 1923 he arrived in Palestine, settling in the new all-Jewish city of Tel Aviv, where he remained until his death in 1934.

Surrounded by fellow Jews who spoke Hebrew, in an atmosphere of hope and confidence in the future of the Jewish people, Bialik continued to write poems, expressing his own and his people's longings and reactions to the events of the day. He established a new publishing house to replace the one that had been closed down in Russia, and together with a lifelong friend and partner, Y. H.

Ravnitzki, he produced a massive anthology of long-forgotten Jewish legends and fables that has become a modern classic.

In Jerusalem a new institution of higher learning—the Hebrew University—was scheduled to open, and Bialik was invited to deliver the principal speech at the dedication exercises. It was a great honor that he always remembered with profound gratitude. Speaking to a crowd of several thousand spectators and guests, many of whom sat on the grass on soil that was permeated with Jewish history, Bialik said, "The eyes of tens of thousands of Israel are lifted from all parts of the world to this hill, shining with hope and comfort. Their hearts and their flesh are singing a blessing of thanksgiving to the living God who has preserved us and sustained us and let us live to see this hour. We must hasten to light here the first lamp of learning and science and of every sort of intellectual activity in Israel, before the lamp grows dark for us in foreign lands."

Bialik's home in Tel Aviv became a center for Jewish leaders from all parts of the world who came to visit Palestine. Although he had broken away from many of the traditional ways in which he had been brought up as a small child, Bialik believed that there were many practices in Jewish tradition that were very worthwhile and deserved to be retained and strengthened.

He introduced the concept of the Oneg Shabbat,

the "Sabbath delight," and it has become an accepted practice in Jewish communities throughout
the world—the idea of spending a few hours on the
Sabbath afternoon to come together with friends
and neighbors, to learn together, sing a little, and
enjoy some light refreshments.

Bialik described his arrival in Palestine as giving
him an opportunity to become one of a "first
generation of free men."

One of the many beautiful poems he composed
is entitled "My Poem":

Would you know from whom, and where I
    learned my song?
A lonesome poet had settled in my father's
    house;
Ever modest, retiring and hidden,
He dwelt in the darkness of cracks and
    crevices.
One melody only this poet knew, one lone
    song, in one familiar style.

But whenever my heart grew sad and
    speechless,
When my tongue clove to my palate in pain,
And a suppressed cry froze in my throat—
He came and filled my empty soul with
    his song.

For he was a cricket, the poet of the poor.

ALEXANDER GOODE
He Gave Up His Life Jacket

OF THE MORE than three hundred rabbis who served as chaplains during World War II, seven lost their lives in service. One of the most unforgettable acts of selflessness and heroism involved Alexander Goode, a rabbi from York, Pennsylvania, who died together with a Catholic priest and two Protestant ministers in an incident that took place in the stormy Atlantic in February of 1943.

The war between the Nazis and the Western world had been going on since 1939 but it was only in December 1941 that America had entered the war, determined to join in the crushing of the Nazis and their Pacific-area partners, the Japanese. In early 1943 the outcome of the war was still in doubt, although the prospects for a victory by the Allies were improving steadily. The Germans were now fighting a two-front war, against the Russians in the east and against the Allies in the west, but they showed little inclination to put down their arms. American transports filled with men and urgently needed supplies formed massive convoys as they steamed into the North Atlantic, intent on providing arms and manpower to the British and, way up north through the port of Murmansk, badly needed supplies for the Russians.

One such transport was the S.S. *Dorchester*, filled to capacity with American troops. On the night of February 3, 1943, a Nazi U-boat fired a torpedo into her side, and within a brief span of time the vessel began to sink. Although all on board had been trained what to do in such an emergency, pandemonium broke loose. Many of the men could not find their life jackets in the dark, and confusion, fear, and hysteria broke out.

In one corner of the vessel four chaplains— Rabbi Goode, Father George L. Fox, Rev. Clark V. Poling, and Rev. John P. Washington—wearing their life jackets, were preparing to board the lifeboats that offered them a chance for survival. And then, almost simultaneously, they realized that scores of young soldiers were running around, bewildered, terrified, because they could not find their own life jackets, and the ship appeared to be ready to sink at any moment. Without any discussion, almost as though they were divinely inspired, all four of the religious leaders removed their life jackets and handed them to the nearest soldiers.

Survivors of that horrible night recall seeing the four men standing on the deck of the doomed vessel, their arms interlocked, almost smiling, not even wishing to take up any room in the crowded lifeboats.

After the war the U.S. government commemorated their action by issuing a postage stamp dedicated to the four chaplains, and one of the permanent exhibits in the Soldiers and Sailors Liberty Memorial Building in Washington comprises the first sheet of the postage stamp. A memorial fountain paying tribute to them was built in the National Memorial Park in Falls Church, Virginia. And a Boy Scout camp in Dillsburg, Pennsylvania, where Rabbi Goode had camped when he was a boy, has erected a memorial chapel.

The heroic four chaplains, including Rabbi Alexander Goode, who gave up their lives so that others might live have become an example of self-sacrificing courageousness that has seldom been matched, an everlasting symbol of faith and heroism above and beyond the call of duty.

YONATAN NETANYAHU
Casualty at Entebbe

THE NAME "ENTEBBE" has come to signify extraordinary courage, heroism, and superior planning and execution. It is the name of an airport in Uganda, in the heart of the African continent, which the world remembers as a place where a few dared to pit their skill and bravery against very heavy odds and emerged triumphant in an unprecedented effort to rescue innocent people in great peril.

The story began to unfold in late June 1976, as the United States was getting ready to celebrate its Bicentennial, the two hundredth anniversary of the founding of the American republic. An Air France airliner was hijacked soon after it took off from Athens on the last leg of what should have been a routine flight from Tel Aviv to Paris. The hijackers were terrorists, mostly Arabs and Germans, and their hostages were Jews and Gentiles. The plane was flown to Entebbe, where the hostages were kept in a virtual prison in an unused airport building. After a few days, the non-Jews were freed and permitted to resume their trip to Paris. The Jews were promised their freedom if the Israel government would free imprisoned Arab terrorists who had been captured in earlier acts of terror.

The world watched with bated breath while the deadline neared when the hostages in Entebbe would either be freed or executed, depending, according to the terrorists, on what the Israel government would do. While some high-ranking diplomats tried to bargain for the release of the hostages and the Israel government reluctantly considered the idea of exchanging their imprisoned terrorists in order to save the lives of the civilian hostages, a top secret plan was being developed for a daring landing at the airport itself and the swift release of the hostages.

To mount such a rescue seemed at first glance almost impossible. Entebbe lay 2,500 miles away from Israel. Reaching the area meant passing through unfriendly territory. Touching down secretly and quickly, snatching the hostages from the hands of their armed captors, and bringing them back safely to Israel—it all seemed more like a fictional plot in a suspense novel than something that could realistically be carried out.

Among the military planners in Israel there were some who believed it could be done and others who thought the idea suicidal. One of the Israeli officers who believed that the plan could work, and that it was well worth the risk in order to save the more than one hundred hostages, was a young lieutenant, Yonatan Netanyahu.

The son of a well-known Israeli scholar, thirty-year-old Yonatan had been born in New York but returned with his family to Israel when he was a small child. Later he returned to New York, and celebrated his bar mitzvah in a Long Beach, New York, synagogue. In the 1967 Six Day War he was an Israeli soldier and was wounded in the fierce fighting on the Golan Heights. Later he chose to enter officers' training school, and during the 1973 Yom Kippur War he was decorated for bravery under fire. It was his unit, under his personal leadership, that was chosen to carry out the daring Entebbe rescue mission, a mission that he felt would succeed and that he also thought had to be carried out, no matter how dangerous, for otherwise it would mean that the State of Israel had turned its back on a group of endangered Jews, who had been spirited off for no reason other than the fact that they were Jews.

The Entebbe rescue mission, which took place in the morning hours of July 4, America's Bicentennial Day, has become a legend. The small convoy that set off from Israel managed to land at the far-off airport, rescue the hostages, and bring them back safely to Israel. Only one member of the rescue team was lost in the raid—Yonatan Netanyahu.

More than four thousand mourners attended the funeral of the young Israeli commando when he was buried at the Mount Herzl Cemetery in Jerusalem. People of good will throughout the world were saddened to learn of his death. In an editorial honoring Israel for its rescue, the *New York Times* said that "it will serve as an inspiration to other countries that, when the occasion demands and if they have the steadfastness and the will, they can do as much."

A book dedicated to young Yonatan's grandfather, a rabbi who died in 1935, spoke of his "life work for Zionism and nobility of spirit." The hero of Entebbe must certainly have inherited some of that dedication to Israel and a measure of that noble spirit.

S. Y. AGNON
Nobel Author with Yarmulke

IN 1966 A MAN wearing a yarmulke and a full dress suit stepped forward as his name was called out and accepted the Nobel Prize for literature—for his own work, and in the name of the people of Israel. Although there had been many Jews who had won the world's most prestigious prize—for physics, chemistry, medicine, and literature—this was the first time an Israeli had been so honored, and it was a day of great rejoicing for Jews everywhere.

Shmuel Yossef Agnon at the time was seventy-eight years old, and he had been writing novels, short stories, poems, and essays almost from the time he was a teenager. Only a few of his books had been translated into English, but the members of the literature prize committee honored Agnon for emerging as a "giant among Israel's writers."

The gentle expression on the old man's face as he received the Nobel Prize was caught in photographs that appeared in newspapers and on television. The expression was a mixture of humaneness, awe, and wonder, blended with his own unique commitment to the ancient principles of the Jewish faith. Agnon, who died a few years later in 1970 in his beloved Jerusalem, personified the man of spirit who sought all his life to illumine the mystery that has guided the destiny of the Jewish people, and the mystique that has dominated the relationship between the Jews and God and between the Jewish people and the Land of Israel.

He was born into a family renowned for its learning, and grew up in a small town in Galicia. The family's name was Czaczkes, but the pen name of Agnon that he adopted later became his permanent name. He studied in local schools, concentrating on traditional biblical and talmudic texts, and was also tutored by his father, who was a fur merchant with a penchant for scholarship. Putting words to paper, in Hebrew and Yiddish, came easily and early to him; and by the time he was fifteen, he had already published a number of poems in both languages. At the age of eighteen he became assistant editor of a Yiddish weekly; and before he was twenty, he set sail for Palestine, settling in Jerusalem, and began to write in earnest.

A year before the outbreak of World War I, in 1913, feeling himself lacking in formal education and sensing the need for greater contact with other literary men, he went to Berlin, where he remained for a decade, returning to Jerusalem in 1924, where he resided the remainder of his life. When he left for Jerusalem, he was accompanied by his wife and two young children. He had studied and worked in Germany, arousing the admiration of various literary critics and winning the support of Zalman Shocken, a distinguished Jewish publisher, who provided him with a steady income so that he could devote all of his time to writing.

Over a span of years his work began to appear in magazines, newspapers, and books, and the students of the Jewish community in Palestine, and later Israel, were taught to read and study his work, which was not always easy to understand. The youngsters, combining the Hebrew initials of his first and middle names, dubbed him "Shai" Agnon and spoke of him with great affection.

Although he was brought up in a home where religious observance was traditional, Agnon for a short time in his life abandoned all Jewish traditions during a period of personal anguish, as a form of protest against what he considered to be the evils that permeated the world. However, this period did not last long, and he became again, and remained, an observant Jew, convinced that the only way the Jewish people could survive and flourish was through a total commitment to their ancient faith.

The Israel Prize for Literature was bestowed on him twice, once in 1954 and again in 1958. Agnon was not the kind of author who sought the limelight, and day in and day out, for a period of many years prior to the establishment of Israel and afterwards, in the difficult days of the fighting of 1948–49, 1956, and 1967, he remained at his desk in his book-lined study in Jerusalem, putting words to paper, creating a world that had existed once in central Europe and another that had flourished in the early years of Palestine, seeking to explain the motivations, the hopes, the frustrations of those bygone days. Many of his stories retain a dream-like quality, and although he was struck by the sense of alienation that many people in the first half of the twentieth century experienced, he was equally convinced that people could achieve a genuine sense of serenity and inner peace if they remained faithful to the basic truths they had been taught that evolved from long centuries of suffering and travail.

Throughout his work Agnon demonstrated that there was an unbreakable kinship between the Jewish people and their ancient homeland. He wrote once about the Western Wall, the only remaining structure from the Holy Temple erected in Jerusalem:

Now the Western Wall is all that we have left of our beloved Temple since ancient times. It has been left by the Holy One, blessed be He, by reason of his great pity for us, and is twelve times as tall as a man, corresponding to the Twelve Tribes, in order that each man in Israel should devote his heart and will to prayer in accordance with his height and his prayer. It is built of great stones, each stone being five ells by six and their like is not to be found in any building in the world. They stand without pitch or mortar or lime between them, in spite of which they are as firmly united as if they were one stone, like the Assembly of Israel which has not even the slightest sovereign power to hold it together, yet is, nonetheless, one unit throughout the world.

When Agnon spoke at the banquet in Stockholm at which he received the Nobel Prize, he said that although he knew it was not so, he nonetheless felt that he had been born in Jerusalem. He said he could trace his ancestry to the ancient Levites, who were the singers and poets of Temple days, and he carried on all his work in that same ancient tradition—writing words that were in effect songs of praise to God.

Reading the works of Agnon requires concentration as well as imagination, for although he himself lived in the twentieth century, he often wrote as though his contemporaries were King

David or Maimonides or Judah the Prince. His writing took little notice of historical facts and sought instead to unite the whole of Jewish history and experience into one tapestry of timelessness.

Many of Israel's younger writers have paid tribute to Agnon for showing them a way to reveal their innermost sentiments, and in that sense one can say that Agnon has laid the groundwork for an exciting new Israeli literature which is only now beginning to be recognized.

HANNAH SENESH
Parachutist with a Mission

ON NOVEMBER 7, 1944, a twenty-three-year-old girl by the name of Hannah Senesh was executed by a firing squad in a prison yard in Budapest, Hungary. Although her Hungarian captors claimed she was an enemy agent parachuted into their country to disrupt their pro-Nazi war efforts, she was a parachutist whose main objective had really been to help her fellow Jews caught up in the web of tyranny and murder that enclosed that hapless country.

Hannah Senesh came from a home that thought of itself as more Hungarian than Jewish. The family discounted the rising tide of anti-Semitic outbreaks in Germany and Austria, but Hannah, then only eighteen, felt that there was no future for Jews except in Palestine. In 1939, leaving her mother's home in Budapest (her father had died earlier), she went to Palestine, where she joined an agricultural settlement. She learned Hebrew, enjoyed the hard work of scrubbing floors and doing the laundry, and would have been happy had it not been for the steady news reports of Nazi victories in one European country after another. She felt especially worried about her mother, who now, like millions of other Jews, was trapped in Nazi-occupied Europe.

She was a shy girl given to writing poetry and filling her diary with her innermost thoughts, but in January of 1943, when she had already become an established settler, she was suddenly struck with one idea: She would somehow get to Hungary, help in any way she could with the underground smuggling of Jews out of the country and into Palestine, and try to include her mother among those who would be brought out. She wrote in her diary about her idea: "It seems absurd, but it is necessary and perhaps possible."

As though by fate, a visitor from a nearby village came to her settlement, announcing that a group of volunteers who were ready to parachute into Europe was being formed. She signed up at once, but it was a whole year before she was finally sent to Egypt for training in a British military center. She passed her training with ease, and in fact found herself reassuring one of the newer recruits. "It is nothing," she said. "You go up in a plane and jump, and immediately you are on the ground again. You'll enjoy it."

She was the first woman volunteer in the parachutist group, and the British officers who were doing the rigorous training and the other young Jews who had volunteered for the dangerous mission were filled with admiration. Her comrades remembered her as tall, blue-eyed, with brown, curly hair flowing about her elongated face. She had seen her brother, Giora, reach haven in Palestine only a short time before she started her parachutist training.

The Palestinian parachutists had all been trained to radio back to British headquarters military information that could be helpful in defeating the Nazis. Their secondary mission was to bring comfort and aid to the beleaguered Jewish communities. On March 13, 1944, the volunteers took off from an Italian airfield and were dropped in Yugoslavia among friendly partisans. Soon after they had settled in with the anti-Nazi fighters, word came that the Nazis had completely taken over Hungary, making entry to that country more difficult than ever. For the next three months, the Palestinian volunteers lived and fought with the partisans in Yugoslavia, Hannah among them. But she counted every day that she was not in Hungary as a wasted day, feeling that if she and her comrades could get to that country, then somehow, perhaps they could do something to help the Jews.

Finally Hannah and two other Palestinians set out to cross the border. It took nearly a month of marching and hiding out in the woods. They crossed the border singly, planning to meet in Budapest, and then suddenly squads of German soldiers and Hungarian police surrounded them all. All were captured and shipped to Gestapo headquarters for questioning. The chief aim of the interrogators was to learn the secret radio code with which the parachutists had planned to help guide British bombers toward their objectives. None of the parachutists, including Hannah, would reveal the code, despite the beatings and various torture methods used by the Germans.

When it was discovered that Hannah was originally a Hungarian and that her mother still lived in Budapest, the police tried to get Hannah to disclose the details of the code by threatening to kill her mother before her eyes, but she could not be swayed. The mother and daughter were reunited briefly in the Budapest prison and fell on each other amid much crying and weeping. Hannah cried out to her mother, "Forgive me, Mother. I had to do it."

Hannah remained in prison for several months. When she was with other Jewish prisoners, she told them about Palestine, encouraging them and setting an example of courage for them. For two months she was confined to a solitary cell, but the jailers could not break her spirit.

Later Hannah's mother was arrested again and kept in the same prison and the two would see each other from a distance, and at times they could converse. Her mother once asked her if she thought her trip by parachute had been worthwhile. Hannah replied, "My time in prison has not been wasted— I have made many Zionists."

Toward the end of her stay in prison Hannah was put back into a large cell with other prisoners, including two small children who had never learned to read or write. She taught them how to do both, and as a reward for their good work made them paper dolls, fashioned from scraps. Her manner was always buoyant, and she undoubtedly helped many of the other prisoners withstand the ordeal of confinement in a Nazi jail.

As the fate of the Nazi war effort became clearer, the Hungarian authorities began to change their attitude toward their prisoners. Hannah's mother was freed, and the one thing she tried desperately to do for her daughter, at Hannah's request, was to obtain for her a Hebrew Bible. Mrs. Senesh scoured all the bookstores and asked dozens of people, but none was to be found. It did not really matter, for in a few days Hannah was transferred to another jail for trial.

Full details of the courtroom proceedings remain unknown, but it has been learned that Hannah stood before her judges and told them defiantly that the Nazis and all their collaborators were a gang of war criminals who would soon be punished for their deeds. The Hungarian judges delayed the verdict for a few days, deeply impressed by the twenty-three-year-old woman from Palestine, and perhaps hoping that the Allies would soon step up their bombing raids or that the Russian forces would soon arrive and put an end to the Nazi regime.

On the morning of November 7 Hannah Senesh stood before a firing squad. The order to shoot was given and her death was instantaneous. Some of the prisoners whispered the traditional Kaddish mourners' prayer for her after hearing the sound of shots. Others, who had come to revere the young woman, remained mute for days on end.

After the war ended, vessels carrying Jewish immigrants to Palestine, mostly survivors of the Nazi concentration camps, fought their way to the shores of the Promised Land, since the British authorities had banned further Jewish immigration. One of these vessels bore the name of Hannah Senesh. It has become, for Israel's young generation, a name synonymous with courage and self-sacrifice.

A gifted poet, Hannah Senesh once wrote:

Happy the match, consumed kindling a flame,
Happy the flame burning in the hidden depths
of hearts.

YIGAL ALLON
Leader of the Palmach

HE REACHED THE PINNACLE of Israeli leadership, serving as his country's foreign minister, consulting with Presidents, Prime Ministers, and world leaders in various fields, and his name was mentioned on a number of occasions as a possible Prime Minister. And yet Yigal Allon was probably most at home in the small farming community where he grew up, nestled at the foot of historic Mount Tabor, where, for his bar mitzvah, his father gave him a gun and said it was time he learned to use it.

He was the youngest of seven brothers, whose mother died when he was still a small child. His father, Reuben Peicovich, was a strong-willed man of the soil who never shrank from a fight although he much preferred the peaceful life of tilling his fields. He was a tough man, and the

117

Arabs who thought they could steal from his farm learned very quickly that he did not hesitate to resist, with gunfire if necessary. In time he won the respect of his Arab neighbors, visited with them, invited them to his home, and tried throughout his lifetime to establish a mutually respectful relationship between his own Jewish community and that of the Arabs.

Yigal grew up on the farm and worked the soil with love and skill. He studied modern farming and applied what he learned, and shared his new knowledge with his friends and neighbors. It was a lonely life, especially after his sister and brothers married and moved elsewhere, but he and his father persisted in the life they had chosen—to make the ancient land fruitful again and to help lay the groundwork for a return of the Jewish people to the homeland.

Like so many other young men in Palestine in the 1920s and 1930s, Yigal Allon became a member of the underground Haganah defense organization. He was sixteen at the time but had already shown traits of leadership, courage, dedication to the cause of Zionism, and expertise with firearms. The Haganah carried out secret training exercises for select young people, and soon Yigal was chosen to be trained for a role as a Haganah officer. He had earlier led a number of patrols against bands of Arab marauders who had been harassing Jewish settlements, and reports of his daring and coolness in action had been sent back to headquarters.

When he was twenty years old, after having been taught the rudiments of modern military tactics, Yigal Allon was given special officers instruction by the Haganah, and made his first contacts with a number of future leaders of Israel, including Moshe Dayan.

A year later, Allon himself became an instructor in a school set up by Haganah for noncommissioned officers. He introduced a concept into the training that has remained a standard exercise for the Israeli defense forces to this day—drills carried out with live ammunition. This, of course, increased the risk of fatalities or wounds, but it also made the young trainees extra vigorous in the course of their training. The Haganah leadership approved his system and soon came to realize that Allon was destined for ever greater responsibilities.

Allon never sent his young volunteers into difficult night forays unless he himself was with them. More than most Palestinian Jews at the time, he felt he understood the Arabs' mentality, and he created the night-attack concept which proved highly effective both in those early years when isolated Haganah units were forced to fight against much larger and better armed Arab units and later when Israel was forced to face Arab armies that outnumbered her men enormously.

When World War II was launched in September 1939 by the German invasion of Poland, thousands of Palestinian Jews—a great many of whom were secret Haganah members—volunteered for service in the British Army. Allon was among the first who wanted to sign up, but his Haganah commanders vetoed the idea. They felt there was a greater need for men of Allon's caliber to remain in Palestine— for one thing, to guard against the possibility of Arab assaults and, for another, to prepare a defense against the possible breakthrough of German troops, whose plan was to seize North Africa, cut through to Egypt, move north to Palestine, and then hold the entire Mediterranean basin in their grip.

Syria and Lebanon in the spring of 1941 actually became pro-Nazi bastions when officials of the Vichy French government took command of those countries. The Haganah leadership even prepared a plan whereby, if the Germans came into Palestine, the Jews would hold out on Mount Carmel in a fortified redoubt from which they would stage surprise sabotage attacks against the enemy.

The uncertainty of the war raging in Europe, North Africa, and the Pacific was so great at the time that the Haganah commanders decided that, in addition to the self-defense Haganah organization, they needed a mobile striking force that could be sent at an instant's notice to any site of Jewish settlement and carry out preemptive attacks in order to avert onslaughts on the Jewish community. Allon was asked to organize such a force, which was named Palmach.

He quickly recruited one hundred Haganah volunteers and, at a special training camp near the Sea of Galilee, set about training a tough, commando-type unit that would be the striking arm of the Jewish community in Palestine. The British knew of the Palmach program and approved. In fact, soon after its formation, Palmach was asked to make its way into Syria and Lebanon to find out the extent of a reported large build-up of pro-Vichy, pro-Nazi troops in the area.

Allon led one group of scouts on a daring operation that prevented a possible massacre of a larger group of Australian soldiers bringing up the rear. The Australian officer in charge was deeply appreciative of the help the Jewish troops had given his men and offered to pay each of the Palmach soldiers. His offer was made through an interpreter since Allon at the time did not understand English. Drawing himself up to his full height, Allon told the interpreter, "Explain that we are not Zulus—we are fighting for our homes, not for money. If we are needed again, we'll be glad to help. After all, we have a common enemy."

In a matter of weeks, the number of Palmach volunteers grew tenfold. The training was tough and merciless. When the British called for volunteers to parachute behind enemy lines into Europe, many of these turned out to be Palmach recruits.

121

They were a very tough, very serious, and very dedicated group of men and women. And the leadership that Allon continued to offer served them as an example and an inspiration.

When the Second World War ended, Palmach soldiers played decisive roles in helping to smuggle thousands of Jews out of Europe to Palestine in the face of British restrictions on Jewish immigration. When Israel was established in May 1948, Yigal Allon was commander of the Palmach, which numbered some seven thousand men. The special force was assigned the most difficult and most dangerous tasks in the war that followed the proclamation of independence, and came through with flying colors.

When peace came, Allon undertook to make up for his lack of formal education. He studied at the Hebrew University and at Oxford, became interested in politics, was elected to the Knesset in 1954 (where he served for many years), became Deputy Prime Minister in 1968 and later Foreign Minister.

Allon liked nothing better than to be able to visit in the home of his Arab neighbor just as he used to do when he was a youngster, converse in Arabic, and cement true bonds of friendship. As a diplomat with a strong military background, however, he was realistic enough to believe that until such a time came, his nation must remain ever vigilant.

He died in 1980.

ROSALYN YALOW
Pioneer of Nuclear Medicine

THE NOBEL PRIZE in medicine for 1977 was bestowed on Dr. Rosalyn Yalow, as well as Dr. Roger Gueillemin and Dr. Andrew Schally. Dr. Yalow is one of the few women doctors or scientists ever to win the prestigious award.

Earlier Dr. Yalow had won the leading American award for medical research, the Lasker Prize. She is a most unusual woman, who combines a seventy-hour work week with the job of caring for her family, maintaining a kosher home, and somehow also managing to take an active part in community Jewish programs.

Born Rosalyn Sussman and raised in the Bronx, the daughter of a traditional family, she received her bachelor's degree from Hunter College in 1941 as that institution's first graduate with a major in physics. At the time few women were allowed to pursue a graduate education in physics; for a while, she had to work as a stenographer, but eventually she was accepted as a student at the University of Illinois and won her doctorate in physics. For more than a quarter of a century she has specialized in research work at the Veterans Administration Hospital in the Bronx. She is head of that institution's department of nuclear medicine and also teaches at the Mount Sinai School of Medicine.

The Nobel Prize was awarded to Dr. Yalow for having perfected a testing procedure that combines "immunology, isotope research, mathematics, and physics." The test is known as the RIA, for radioimmunoassay. It is so sensitive that it can detect the billionth part of a gram. As one member of the Nobel Prize committee explained it, the RIA is like finding a lump of sugar in a lake sixty-two miles wide, sixty-two miles long, and thirty feet deep.

Dr. Yalow is quick to pay tribute to her late colleague Dr. Solomon Berson for the successful conclusion of her work, described by the Nobel Prize authorities as being of major significance to practically every area of medicine. When the test that Drs. Yalow and Berson developed was described in a scientific paper, it was rejected by the editor of a leading medical journal, who subsequently had reason to regret his decision.

Doctors carrying out diagnoses of their patients

are now able to detect what may seem like trivial changes in their patients' hormones, which can in turn produce radical effects on their health. The new method of testing and evaluation continues to lead to new discoveries and understanding of the nature of the human body.

The RIA is already in use by thousands of blood collection centers to prevent the inclusion of blood contaminated with hepatitis. Cancer research programs also are making extensive use of the new testing procedure.

During the many years that the testing procedures were developed, both Dr. Yalow and Dr. Berson made themselves available as guinea pigs, acting as volunteers for testing of the thyroid, blood, and albumin.

Dr. Yalow's husband, Aaron, whose father was a leading rabbi in Syracuse, New York, for many years, is a professor of physics. Their son, Ben, is a computer systems analyst, and their daughter, Elanna, is doing her doctoral work for a career in educational psychology.

At the Bronx VA hospital, Dr. Yalow is admired by her colleagues and by the young students who help her in her work. Sometimes she takes time out to prepare meals for her staff at the hospital, as well as doing the same for her family. She explains her ability to carry a full work load by the fact that she is thoroughly organized, and depends at home on a big freezer and a microwave oven.

Dr. Yalow was the first American woman ever to receive a Nobel Prize in science. Her vigorous and optimistic approach to her daily work routine make it seem likely that she will continue to develop important new advances in medical science.

SHALOM ALEICHEM
The Jewish Mark Twain

TENS OF MILLIONS of people throughout the world have seen and enjoyed a musical play and film called *Fiddler on the Roof*, which depicts the life of Jews in eastern Europe about a century ago with deep understanding. The show is based on the writings of Shalom Aleichem, the pen name of Solomon Rabinowitz, a Jewish literary genius whose talent came to be appreciated mostly after his death in the Bronx, New York, in 1916.

He was born in a small town in Russia, similar to the famous village of Kasrilevke depicted in *Fiddler on the Roof*. From his earliest days he showed a special talent for writing (and also acting) in a humorous vein, and he sensed that humor could cover up, at least temporarily, pain and suffering. Unlike most Jewish youths in Russia at the time, he received a good general as well as

127

Jewish education, and for a while he served as a tutor and even a rabbi. He was a prolific writer, and because he enjoyed writing for large numbers of people, he turned to the Yiddish language in order to reach the largest possible number of Jewish readers. His father was a lover of Hebrew, and to avoid being harassed for writing in Yiddish, the young man adopted the pen name of Shalom Aleichem—an expression literally meaning "Peace be unto you," used as a common greeting rather like "How do you do?"

His literary efforts attracted a large and growing audience, and people used to refer to Shalom Aleichem as a jester who understood their everyday needs and problems. Earning money was always a problem for him, and it was not until after his father-in-law's death, when he inherited a sizable estate, that he was able to live comfortably, at least for a while.

Shalom Aleichem has been called "the Jewish Mark Twain," and he too, like the great American humorist, was a poor businessman and lost large sums of money in unsound investments. Twain (who once referred to himself as "the American Shalom Aleichem") learned how easy it was to reduce his financial worth through investing in a mechanical typesetting machine, while Shalom Aleichem thought of himself as a sharp speculator on the stock exchange who could make a fortune by clever investments. At one point, things got so bad that Shalom Aleichem had to flee his home in Russia, hiding out from creditors until all his debts were paid off by his mother-in-law.

Nonetheless, he remained an eternal optimist and saw life through lenses ground from humor. He continued to write steadily—novels, plays, stories, essays—and his work appeared in Yiddish newspapers in Russia, Poland, America, and elsewhere, and everywhere readers loved him, for he brought smiles and tears of joy to their otherwise drab and often difficult lives. His financial difficulties however were with him most of his life. When he died in New York, his funeral procession was accompanied by hundreds of thousands of Jewish factory workers who took time off from their jobs to pay him their last respects, but he died virtually a pauper.

Shalom Aleichem created a lovable character, Mottele, the cantor's son, who—like Mark Twain's unforgettable hero Huckleberry Finn—becomes an orphan and has to find his own way in life. Mottele's milieu was the small village of the East European Jews, which he described with love and wonder notwithstanding the poverty and the ceaseless struggle to maintain some kind of order and dignity in an abysmal world.

Shalom Aleichem, in all his work, seemed to hold up a mirror to the hundreds of thousands of Jews of eastern Europe in which he showed them that, despite their difficulties, they had much to be grateful for and that their lives could be more bearable if they approached their problems with a smile and a laugh. To paraphrase the old Yiddish expression, he helped to make his readers laugh through their own tears.

In recent years a whole new generation of readers has begun to appreciate what a kind, understanding, and keen writer Shalom Aleichem really was. His works have been translated into Hebrew, Russian, English, and many other languages. A literary center in Tel Aviv bears his name.

In the latter years of his life, Shalom Aleichem allied himself with the Zionist movement and even attended one of the World Zionist Congress meetings as an official delegate. Still writing tirelessly, he also expended much time and energy traveling to communities all over Russia and Poland before World War I, giving readings of his works in order to increase his earnings. The travels he was forced to engage in eventually undermined his health, and he contracted tuberculosis.

He died at the age of fifty-seven, leaving the world a richer place for his wise and loving understanding of the Jewish people he loved so profoundly.

YIGAEL YADIN
He'd Rather Dig Than Fight

YIGAEL YADIN was a reluctant military leader. He much preferred to devote his time to his primary vocation and avocation — archaeology. He was one of the world's foremost figures in this field, certainly the leading archaeologist of Israel.

He was born in Jerusalem in 1917, the son of a famous professor of archaeology, Eliezer Sukenik. At the age of fifteen he became a scout for the Haganah, the secret underground army of the Jewish community in Palestine, then governed by the British. He knew that sooner or later a Jewish state would be created in Palestine, and he was anxious to participate fully in realizing the age-old dream of the Jewish people.

He rose in the ranks of the organization and by 1947 was named operations officer. When Israel proclaimed its independence in 1948, the then

131

Chief of Staff, Yaacov Dori, who had been the head of Haganah, was confined to a hospital and Yadin became Chief of Staff, working closely with David Ben-Gurion, the Prime Minister, to assure that the infant nation would not go under in the large-scale fighting that followed the attacks of neighboring Arab countries.

In 1952 Yadin, now a general, resigned from the Israel Defense Forces to devote himself to scholarship, especially in the field of archaeology. It was as though he personally wanted to be transformed, in the spirit of Isaiah, from a sword into a plowshare. One of his principal contributions to the security of Israel was the introduction of the system of conscription and reserves, a system that has enabled Israel to withstand the far greater numbers of soldiers found in the Arab countries.

He resumed his studies at the Hebrew University and in 1955 received a doctorate for his work on explaining the origin, background, and significance of some of the Dead Sea Scrolls, manuscripts preserved intact for centuries hidden in an inaccessible cave near the Dead Sea. The following year he was awarded the Israel Prize for his work.

As an archaeologist, Yadin was anxious to link the ancient past of the Jewish people in Israel with the present. Employing thousands of volunteers, he directed an excavation of a once great city, Hazor, located north of the Sea of Galilee, over a period of five years. In antiquity Hazor had been a major center, inhabited at different times by the Israelites under Joshua and by Canaanites, Persians, Greeks, and other peoples. Strategically sited, it was always known as a fortress city.

Using the Bible as a guide, Yadin and his teams began to dig, gradually peeling back layer upon layer of ancient civilizations, excavating invaluable artifacts, and finally finding evidence of the great battle waged against Hazor by Joshua in the thirteenth century B.C.E. The diggers found courtyards, chariots, staircases, reservoirs, jugs, pots, letters, temples, and palaces. For an archaeologist like Yadin, these finds were a glorious adventure back into the long-forgotten past.

A few years later Yadin led an expedition to the cliffs of Ein Gedi, looking for hard evidence of the existence of Simeon Bar Kochba, who led a rebellion against the Romans after the Holy Temple had been destroyed in the year 70. To enter the caves in the area, it was necessary to fly army helicopters to hover directly above the narrow entrances, lower a volunteer from a rope, let him swing back and forth like a pendulum, and then hope he would succeed in throwing himself into the slit entrance of the ancient, foul-smelling cave. The operation worked, and, among other valuable finds, the archaeologists came upon fifteen letters from Bar Kochba to his lieutenants, issuing orders for the continued military campaign against the hated Romans. The announcement by Yadin of the discovery of the documents was made at the residence of the President of Israel, and electrified the world.

In 1964 Yadin turned his attention to the natural fortress of Masada, a flat-topped mountain south of the Dead Sea, shaped like a ship, with practically vertical sides. It is a breath-taking place to visit, and today future officers of the Israel Defense Forces are brought there to take their oath of loyalty to Israel.

Masada is best known in Jewish history for the courage of a group of fewer than a thousand men, women, and children who encamped there following the Roman victory over the Jews, determined to continue to offer resistance, no matter how high the cost. The Roman soldiers surrounding the fortress began to build a huge ramp from which they would be able to send their soldiers into the Jewish stronghold and crush the rebels. Day by day the Romans brought earth and packed it tight, and the ramp continued to grow higher and higher. The leader of the besieged Jews, Eleazar ben Yair, knew that it was only a matter of time before the Romans would overrun the Jewish encampment.

According to the ancient historian Josephus, Eleazar called his followers together and told them, "Let us die unenslaved by our enemies, and leave this world as free men, together with our wives and children."

He outlined a grisly plan: Ten men would act as executioners and would go about killing every man, woman, and child on Masada and then execute each other. The last man to remain alive would be instructed to inspect the bodies making sure that all were lifeless, and then to take his own life.

When the Roman soldiers finally broke into Masada, they were sickened by what they saw: With the exception of one old woman and five small children who had remained hidden in a water conduit, all were dead. The message of zealousness for freedom had been made painfully clear.

Under Yadin's leadership, teams of volunteers set about to uncover the whole historic tableau. They dug up an ancient palace built by King Herod, complete with the throne room, reception halls, servants' quarters, and workshops. Mosaic floors installed centuries ago had stood the test of time and were clearly visible.

The Masada zealots had burned down everything they could before carrying out their mass suicide, and apparently the ashes that remained had helped preserve the artifacts of the time. Yadin's teams found ancient coins, letters, arrows, and even the skeletons of the martyrs. Jars containing food were uncovered, as were the ancient baths, bedecked with beautiful frescoes.

In the living quarters, the diggers came upon various household utensils—stoves, basins, dishes. Here and there sandals lay scattered about. A

mikveh, a ritual bath, and the remains of a synagogue were found, too.

In 1965 Masada was dedicated as a national
shrine in Israel. The watchword "Masada shall not
fall again" became a national slogan.

Yadin's work has been acclaimed throughout
the world, for he succeeded in shedding light on
what had been a lost chapter in Jewish history. At
his initiative, a peculiarly shaped building known
as the Shrine of the Book has been established near
the Israel Museum in Jerusalem, in which are kept
the fragments of the Dead Sea Scrolls, as well as
some of the Bar Kochba letters and other ancient
artifacts.

In 1977 Yadin, who earlier had formed a new
political party in Israel, the Democratic Movement
for Change, was named Deputy Prime Minister.

He died in 1984.

I. I. RABI
Nuclear Energy for Peace

HE SERVED as chairman of the Science Advisory Committee under President Dwight Eisenhower. In 1944 he was awarded the Nobel Prize in physics for his discovery of the resonance method of determining the magnetic properties of the atomic nucleus. For a number of years he led the advisory committee of the Atomic Energy Commission, and he is today one of the most respected men of science in the world.

Isidore Isaac Rabi, usually known by the initials of his first and middle names, was brought to the United States as a small child and grew up in a poor home. His father was a grocer and had worked for a time in a dress factory. After graduating from a New York high school, young Rabi was awarded a scholarship at Cornell University and earned a degree in chemistry in three years. For the next few years he worked at a variety of jobs, trying to decide exactly what to do, and then he resumed his graduate work, first at Cornell and later at Columbia, in physics, supporting himself as a tutor at City College.

He had switched from chemistry to physics, and his special expertise in this area won him a chance to travel to Europe to work and study with some of the great physicists of the time—Bohr, Stern, Heisenberg, and Pauli. He became fascinated by the new field of molecular beams, especially as it was related to the measurements of atomic magnetism.

He joined the Columbia physics faculty, and has been part of the famous university's innovative physics department since 1927. In 1977 he was honored for a half century of teaching physics at Columbia, which has turned out one quarter of all the American Nobel laureates in physics.

Like many immigrants to the United States, Rabi has always had a deep attachment to his new country. He became interested in helping in the defense of the United States at about the same time that the Nazis rose to power in Germany. Soon after war broke out in Europe, he divided his time between his teaching duties at Columbia and a project being carried out secretly at MIT in Cambridge, Massachusetts, that led to the development of military radar. Simultaneously he was also involved in the top-secret Manhattan Project, which led to the creation of the first atomic bomb.

When the Nobel Prize was awarded to Rabi in 1944, the war was still raging and he did not deliver the traditional lecture in Stockholm. He was too involved with the work he was doing for the U.S. military at the time anyway; a few years later the defense department awarded him the Medal of Merit, honoring him for "exceptional meritorious conduct in the performance of outstanding service to the United States, from November 1940 to December 1945, as consultant to many key defense organizations, [and for maintaining] the highest level of inspirational initiative in the application of scientific techniques to military problems."

The distinguished scientist also took a deep interest in the development of a number of important scientific institutions in Israel, especially the Technion-Israel Institute of Technology and the Weizmann Institute of Science. He loaned his name to a number of organizations that were working in behalf of Israel, and visited that country a number of times, offering his services as a mentor in various phases of scientific development.

A decade after the first atomic bomb was dropped on Hiroshima, Rabi was one of the principal figures in a worldwide Atoms for Peace Conference convened in Geneva under United Nations auspices. Like other distinguished nuclear scientists, he was fearful of the misuse of atomic energy and tried to use his influence to reducing its easy accessibility and potential for destruction.

Although he has received the highest honors and accolades that can be given, Rabi has remained an essentially modest man, anxious to learn and teach, trying to see the bright side of things, hoping that the world's entrance into the atomic age will bring with it an era of peace and prosperity but mindful that there are very real dangers of unscrupulous individuals or governments appropriating the new force for their own, diabolical ends.

Of the first detonation of the atomic bomb in the New Mexico desert, Rabi has written:

> The atomic age came at about five-thirty in the morning of July 16, 1945. It was a sight which I have attempted from time to time to describe. I never felt successful in doing it. One has to go back to the Bible, to witnesses of the ancient miracles, to get some impression of the tremendous emotional experience it produced. . . . Many things can be done which were quite impossible up to now. Very important developments in chemistry, particularly in biological chemistry and medicine, will be brought about. We will be able to learn things which we could not find out before. We have a real revolution ahead of us through the use of [radioactive] materials.

The diversion of nuclear energy to peaceful, helpful, life-saving goals has become the primary objective of the distinguished Nobel laureate in physics.

ELIEZER BEN-YEHUDA
Father of Modern Hebrew

PEOPLE USED TO CALL HIM a fanatic, but that didn't trouble him. He was a man obsessed with a dream unlike any other dream or any other man: He believed that the future of the Jewish people would be immeasurably strengthened if there were once again one common language, the ancient biblical language of Hebrew, that bound Jews together, and he set about to turn his dream into reality. Amazingly, he succeeded. Ben-Yehuda is believed to be the only man in history who ever revived a language of ancient times and made it again a living, spoken tongue.

He was born in 1858 in Lithuania, and his family name was originally Perelmann. He changed it to reflect the ancient method of using one's father's first name as a family name when he left for Palestine in 1881. When he and his young bride, Devorah, set foot on the soil of the ancient Jewish homeland, then under the control of harsh Turkish authorities, he told her from that moment on they would never again speak anything but Hebrew—and he was true to his word.

Their son, Itamar, was raised in the first Hebrew-speaking home of modern times, and because the other children of the Jewish community, made up largely of Orthodox Jewish families, spoke only Yiddish, reserving the use of Hebrew for prayer and study of the Bible and Talmud, the youngster had a hard time making friends.

Ben-Yehuda ignored all of his opponents who said the idea of reviving Hebrew was a wild scheme. The ultra-Orthodox Jews claimed it was blasphemous to use a holy tongue like Hebrew for everyday needs, while even some of the Zionist leaders expressed grave doubts that the idea could ever possibly work. Jews at the time spoke Yiddish, Russian, German, and in the case of Sephardic Jews, Ladino. True, they all knew Hebrew from their prayers and Bible study, but nobody actually spoke or wrote the language.

Nevertheless, Ben-Yehuda persisted. He said that sooner or later Jews would leave the Diaspora because of violent or nonviolent anti-Semitism or because of the threat of assimilation into the mainstream of their respective lands of exile, and they would need a common language to help form a united people. Reviving Hebrew, he insisted, not only would give them that language but also would serve as a bridge between the days of the Temple—some two thousand years past—and the present time, buttressing their right to return to the ancient Jewish homeland.

When he first arrived in Jerusalem, Ben-Yehuda found that most of the Jews there were ultra-Orthodox, who knew Hebrew well from their daily prayers and Bible study. He decided to try to win them over to transforming Hebrew into a daily, spoken language, and to accomplish this, he began to act the role of an Orthodox Jew.

He grew a beard and sidecurls and persuaded his wife to wear a *sheitel*, a wig worn by Orthodox women. The subterfuge did not work, however, when the Orthodox Jews saw that Ben-Yehuda was trying to turn Hebrew from a purely holy tongue into one of mundane use. They soon turned against him, and he subsequently became a lifelong opponent of religious fanaticism.

He took a job as a teacher in a Jerusalem school run by the Alliance Israelite Universelle and succeeded in introducing the teaching of Hebrew, at least for courses in Judaica. It was a beginning, and soon thereafter he launched a Hebrew-language weekly newspaper, which struggled with each issue to introduce new words to describe developments and objects that could not even have been imagined in biblical times. He always sought to coin new words that had their origin in ancient

Hebrew words or roots, although at times he was forced to adopt terms from foreign languages.

His wife died in 1891, and he married her younger sister, Hemda, who was destined to spend a lifetime raising funds for his magnum opus—a Hebrew dictionary that would encompass all words from the ancient past to the present day. Ben-Yehuda devoted all his time to inculcating his concept of a revived Hebrew language among all sectors of the nascent Zionist movement, as well as to his dictionary and his newspaper.

At one time Ben-Yehuda was imprisoned for allegedly having written an editorial in his newspaper calling for a revolt against the Turkish authorities. The utterly false accusation had been instigated by a number of the older Jerusalemite Jews who were bitterly opposed to his "heretical" ways. His jailing actually helped his work, since most segments of the younger Jewish community came to realize that his cause was just and rallied to his defense, in effect aligning themselves with his efforts on behalf of Hebrew.

A critical situation developed for Ben-Yehuda in the early 1920s, when "the war of the languages" broke out. Influential and wealthy German Jews had decided to establish a technical school in Haifa and insisted that the language of instruction be German. A number of the teachers in the new school and early leaders of the Zionist movement then living in Palestine urged Ben-Yehuda to rally a campaign against the use of German. It became a cause célèbre, with student and teacher strikes, popular petitions, and appeals to influential Jewish leaders in Europe. Eventually, the conflict was resolved, and Hebrew won out as the language of instruction in the new technical school (originally called the Technikum and later Hebraized to Technion). The linguistic victory became the watershed that led to a growing use of Hebrew in all schools in the country.

Ben-Yehuda took no time out for victory celebrations, always mindful of the dictionary project he was working on. He traveled with his wife to London and other European capitals, where he immersed himself in scholarly libraries, seeking clues to long-forgotten Hebrew terms, while his wife met with local philanthropists and Zionist supporters, seeking financial aid for the dictionary her husband was preparing.

When the first volumes appeared, they created a sensation in the philological and scholarly worlds. There, in black and white, Ben-Yehuda had succeeded in listing words and idioms that had been all but buried in the Bible, the Talmud, and other religious and legal works dating back many centuries. The dictionary was thick with Jewish history and geography, and Ben-Yehuda's achievement was immediately hailed by scholars.

A Language Academy was formed in Jerusalem, in which scholars began to contribute their

own words—sometimes coined, sometimes redis-
covered from ancient sources—to the growing
old-new language. Ben-Yehuda was deeply involved with that, too.

The massive multivolume dictionary was not
completed at the time of his death in 1922, but
Ben-Yehuda lived to hear Hebrew beginning to be
spoken on all sides of him as the size of the Jewish
community in Palestine continued to grow. His
son, Ehud, carried on his father's dictionary project,
and in 1959 the entire seventeen volume work
appeared, a vast and vital contribution to Hebrew
learning and lexicography.

Hebrew today is spoken not only by the more
than three and a half million Jewish citizens of
Israel but also by scores of thousands of non-Jews
living in the country. A major part of the curricu-
lum of Jewish religious schools in all parts of the
world includes the teaching of Hebrew, not only
for prayers but also for use as a language of
everyday life. In the United States, England,
Canada, and a number of other countries Hebrew
is offered as a full-fledged foreign language on
college campuses as well as in some high schools.
There are even Hebrew-speaking summer camps
in various parts of the United States. Conversely,
the study of Hebrew was banned until recently in
the Soviet Union, a prohibition that has led many
thousands of Soviet Jews to study the language
from secretly home-produced texts.

Although Hebrew has not become as widespread or popular as English or French, a great joy was felt among all lovers of the language when the Israeli author S. Y. Agnon, who wrote in Hebrew, was awarded the Nobel Prize in literature.

The Hebrew language, like all modern tongues, is a living, organic entity, and the Language Academy is still busy coining new words, seeking wherever possible to base these on ancient terms.

Ben-Yehuda's dream of a reborn Hebrew language to help unite the Jews returning to Israel has been realized. Jewish immigrants from Rumania, England, North Africa, Latin America, and many other countries—where both Yiddish and Ladino have been on the wane—now study Hebrew in intensive courses and can meet each other on the common ground of a common language, thanks to Ben-Yehuda's vision and determination.

DAVID BEN-GURION
Architect of Israel

HE WAS ACKNOWLEDGED as the architect and principal founder of the State of Israel and served the new nation as Prime Minister and Minister of Defense. He could be charming and tough; he read the Bible assiduously and could quote at random lengthy passages, particularly from the book of Isaiah; and because he admired the early Greek philosophers and was not satisfied to read them in translation, taught himself ancient Greek and studied the works of Plato, Socrates, and Aristotle in the original.

He was born in 1886 in Plonsk, at the time in Russian-held Poland, the son of an ardent Zionist whose family name was Gruen (Ben-Gurion later Hebraized his surname). His mother died when he was eleven, and young David received a relatively modern Hebrew and secular education, much of it

151

from private tutors. When he was fourteen he was already involved with an early Zionist group and began to travel around Poland, calling for adherence to a Zionist answer to the problems of the Jewish community. In 1905 the authorities arrested him, but his father managed to obtain his release, and the next year Ben-Gurion left for Palestine.

He earned a living picking oranges in Petah Tikvah and working in the wine cellars of Rishon le-Zion. Palestine at the time was part of the Ottoman Empire and Ben-Gurion and his lifelong friend Yitzhak Ben-Zvi, who later became Israel's second President, decided to enroll in Turkish universities to study law and try to establish better relations between the small Jewish community then in Palestine and the Turkish leaders. The two young students were arrested instead and deported to Egypt; within a year they set sail for the United States to help expand the Zionist movement there.

In 1917 Ben-Gurion met and married a New York nurse, Paula Munweis, herself an ardent labor Zionist. In the same year the British government issued the Balfour Declaration, expressing its support for the establishment of a Jewish homeland in Palestine, and the next year a Jewish Legion was formed to help defeat the German and Turkish forces. Ben-Gurion was one of the early volunteers for the Legion, and arrived in Egypt in May, as part of a contingent attached to the British army.

When the war ended, he proceeded to Palestine and threw himself into the political work that he hoped would lay the groundwork for a Jewish state based on socialist principles, especially on the credo of the kibbutz movement. For a decade he was an active leader of the Histadrut, and in the early 1930s he became more closely identified with the official Zionist movement. He became chairman of the Jewish Agency executive in 1935 in effect sharing the leadership of the worldwide Zionist movement with its president, Chaim Weizmann.

In 1939 the British government announced a sharp curtailment of Jewish immigration to Palestine, despite the deteriorating situation of European Jewry in a continent in which the forces of Hitlerism were on the upsurge. Ben-Gurion led the Jewish community's denunciation of the new policy and called for resistance to it as well as expansion of so-called illegal immigration of Jews to Palestine.

At the conclusion of World War II he visited the displaced persons camps where scores of thousands of former inmates of Nazi camps and ghettos were waiting for an opportunity to emigrate from blood-soaked Europe. In his fiery manner, he told the Jewish survivors of Nazism, "We shall not rest until every one of you who so desires joins us in the land of Israel in building a Jewish state." He directed all-out efforts to help bring as many of the refugees to Palestine as possible, even if it meant using unseaworthy vessels. At the same time, he ordered the leaders of Haganah, the Jewish defense organization, to start acquiring arms, for he felt that sooner or later the Arabs surrounding the Jewish community in Palestine would mount a full-fledged attack.

In November 1947 the United Nations voted to establish a Jewish and an Arab state in Palestine. A month later, armed Arab attacks against Jewish settlements began, which were escalated when the State of Israel was proclaimed on May 14, 1948. Although he had able military people around him— including the American volunteer Colonel David ("Mickey") Marcus—in essence Ben-Gurion in his role as Defense Minister directed the war effort, in the same manner and spirit as Churchill had done in England a few years earlier.

The proclamation of independence was not something desired by all of the Jewish leaders at the time. Some felt Israel was too weak; others said waiting for a more propitious moment would be more practical. Ben-Gurion overruled all objections, saying that the Jews had waited nearly two thousand years to re-establish the Jewish homeland, and after the bitter years of the Hitler era and the postwar suffering of the survivors of the Holocaust, the time had come for such a step.

On a Friday afternoon, in great secrecy, the leaders of the Jewish community of Palestine gathered in Tel Aviv and solemnly pronounced the establishment of the State of Israel. Ben-Gurion was named the first Prime Minister, and within a few minutes of the announcement, transmitted worldwide by radio, the United States became the first country to recognize the new state.

In the proclamation of Israel's independence, the country was described as the

land where the Jewish people came into being. In this land was shaped their spiritual, religious and national character. Here they created a culture of national and universal import and gave to the world the eternal Book of Books.... The State of Israel will be open to Jewish immigration and the ingathering of the exiles.

While crowds of exuberant men, women, and children cheered and danced in the streets of Tel Aviv and Jerusalem, Arab armies proceeded to try to crush the new state in its very infancy. For the next few years, Ben-Gurion labored mightily, supervising first the defense of the country and then the task of integrating the huge shiploads and planeloads of Jews who began to stream into Israel. He served in his dual capacity as Prime Minister and Defense Minister for five years, and then after a hiatus of two years, resumed his old job for a stint of eight more years.

In 1963 he left government service and retired

to a spartan life on a kibbutz in the Negev, hoping no doubt that his example of settling in a remote corner of Israel would be emulated by others. He devoted himself to writing a history of the rebirth of Israel and to pursuing his own prodigious reading and study.

During the period that he helped fashion Israel, the country's Jewish population rose from less than three quarters of a million at the time of the proclamation of independence to more than two and a half million when he stepped down from office (it is today more than three and a half million). Agriculture, industry, education, defense, housing—virtually all areas of the life of a modern nation—grew during his tenure of office. He visited with the leaders of several west European countries to cement better ties between Israel and the older, more established democracies. He conferred with President John Kennedy, and often spoke to Jewish fundraising meetings in America. One of his most dramatic tours of the United States took place when he flew around the country in a chartered plane, helping to launch the Israel Bonds program.

When he died in 1973, Jews throughout the world felt that the founding father of Israel was no more.

Janus Korczak
Physician of the Children

AT FIRST GLANCE, his is not even a Jewish name. And then, it seems hardly pronounceable. Yet, so long as men and women continue to admire moral courage and a heart brimming with kindness, the name of this remarkable man—pronounced *ya' noosh kor'chak*—will live on. If Jews had a system of saints, he would certainly be high on the list of candidates for canonization.

His real name was Henryk Goldszmidt, but he was so well known as an author of books for children and a writer on children for educators and parents under the name of Korczak that that is how he is best remembered today.

The exact date of his birth is not certain, although it was probably 1878. The family into which he was born was wealthy and assimilationist, and if you were to ask its members, all of them ardent patriots of Poland, if they were Jews or Poles, the immediate response would be the latter.

Young Henryk grew up in comfortable circumstances and chose to become a physician. The terrible condition of the poor, especially the orphans, of Poland in the early years of this century moved him to help them improve their lot. First, the young doctor volunteered his services as a social worker—physician in a summer camp for underprivileged children, and later he was named director of a Jewish orphanage in Warsaw.

In those days, orphanages were large, impersonal, often cruel institutions run by apathetic people who were not really interested in the children's welfare. Discipline was tight, and boys and girls would line up with their spoons and bowls into which hot food was ladled—like some scene out of a Dickens novel—and that would be a major part of the care extended.

The idealistic, compassionate young doctor saw that the system was all wrong, and set about changing it. He introduced a method whereby the children themselves were given responsibility for running the orphanage, feeling that they would then not have to be reminded about such prosaic subjects as cleanliness, manners, and decorum. His innovations were then unique, and he began to write about them in the hope they would be emulated by other orphanage directors for the benefit of the parentless children.

The young charges in Korczak's care realized very quickly that this was no ordinary man who had come to run the institution but a sympathetic, warm human being who really had their best interests at heart. Unfailingly he dealt with each child as though he were indeed his or her father, sometimes teaching, sometimes scolding gently, always encouraging the youngsters to understand that they had an opportunity to improve their station in life through serious study, genuine interest in other people, and a code of high moral standards.

To say that the orphans in his care loved him and he loved them in turn would be an understatement. In the wee hours of the night he would sit and write imaginative stories for children, about a world in which the government was run by children—children who knew no guile and who practiced what was right and just without reference to "practical" considerations. His stories were of a mythical kingdom, but they expressed his strong belief that boys and girls were basically pure of heart and if given a chance could do a better job of running the world than the adults had been doing for as long as people could remember.

Typical of the books that he wrote for educators and parents, long before similar approaches began to be taken by modern innovators in pedagogy, were *How to Love a Child* and *The Child's Right to Respect*.

From 1911 until the beginning of the Nazi

invasion of Poland in 1939, Korczak ran his orphanage, through which passed thousands of children during that span of almost three decades. His pioneering, far-sighted methods won him a wide reputation, and social workers and others came to visit and observe his institution from many parts of the world.

The strong Jewish identity he had missed in his own youth had gradually taken hold of him as he dealt on a daily basis with the youngsters in his care. He became interested in the kibbutz movement in Palestine and went there to observe and study, expressing his admiration for the way the children of the kibbutz were being treated and raised. The Jewish leaders of Palestine, sensing no doubt that here was a rare man who could help them fashion an even better system for caring for their youngsters, urged him to stay on in Palestine, but he declined, explaining that he was needed in the orphanage in Warsaw. He returned to Poland, although the Nazi war clouds were already visible.

Korczak never married, and thus devoted all of his time to the children in his care. If anything, his gentleness and patience seemed to grow with each passing year. In 1942, after the total collapse of Polish resistance to the German invaders, he and his two hundred young orphans were forcibly removed from the building they occupied and herded into a section of the Warsaw ghetto, where they lived among an estimated 300,000 other imprisoned Jews. Like so many other Jews in the ghetto, Korczak heard rumors of what the Germans were doing to the Jews trapped in Nazi dominated territory but refused, at first at least, to believe these incredible reports.

Conditions in the Warsaw ghetto gradually grew worse. Hunger and disease were everywhere, and in the winter months there was no fuel for heating or cooking.

And then one day one of the Jewish policemen employed by the Nazis, a member of a hated group who sought to save themselves by helping the Germans, knocked on the door of Korczak's apartment. His eyes were bleary and red-rimmed, betraying his drunkenness. Tears in his eyes, he told the director of the orphanage that he had learned that Korczak's orphans were scheduled to be deported the next day. Taking a deep swallow from a flask in his hand, the informer begged Korczak not to reveal that he had been notified in advance.

By now Korczak was convinced that the reports of the deliberate extermination of the Jews caught in the Nazi trap were true. He did not know what to do, where to turn. Should he tell his young wards that in a matter of days or weeks or months they would all be dead? Dared he panic them, frighten them more than they were already frightened? Should he try to help them somehow to escape, or put up some resistance in the hope that at least some of them would evade the fate that now seemed so clear to him awaited them all? Or should he perhaps try to make their last hours on earth as enjoyable as possible, by an act of deceit?

The dilemma tormented him until he finally decided what he must do. With a forced smile on his lips, he summoned the children and announced that the next day they would all go on a picnic. He told them to put on their best Sabbath clothes and get a good rest that night. The children were delighted.

The next morning, the informer's tip was proven right. All the people on the block, including the two hundred orphans, were rounded up and taken in sealed trucks to a railway station outside the walls. Korczak assured the children that all was well, that they were merely getting a train ride out into the country.

At the station, before the Jews were ordered into the cattle cars that would transport them to the Treblinka death camp, one of the Nazi officials, aware of Korczak's worldwide reputation as an educator, offered to release him, but the doctor refused.

Wearing their best clothes, the whole group, led by Korczak carrying a very small child in his arms, entered the train. They were never seen again.

The governments of both Israel and Poland have issued postage stamps bearing the saddest expression ever seen on a man's face—that of

Janus Korczak, who loved all children and who lived to see a world in which fellow human beings deliberately exterminated his beloved children because they were Jewish. The look on his face will eternally haunt humanity.

ELI COHEN
A Spy Who Died for Israel

THE WORD "SPY" has a sinister connotation. One thinks of shadowy figures lurking in the dark, doing things that are not legal in order to serve their respective countries. Eli Cohen was a spy in the service of Israel, but he was anything but a sinister person. He grew up in Egypt, and from his early youth he dreamed of being able to emigrate to Israel and join his coreligionists in building a Jewish state that would be an example of a modern, progressive, democratic nation steeped in the ancient biblical teachings of the prophets.

He was born in 1924 but it was not until 1957, when he was thirty-three years old, that he managed to make his way to Israel. He was now married and had a family, and he felt that he was being given a second chance in life, for he found that he loved every aspect of Israel even more than he had dared dream when he was a youngster.

One day he was approached by a representative of the Israeli military intelligence service. The man said that Israel desperately needed to know what was going on in some of the Arab countries, so that there would be no chance of any sudden, sneak attacks. He explained to Cohen that the intelligence service knew that he was a loyal Jew, deeply devoted to Israel, that he spoke and knew Arabic fluently, that he could pass for an Arab. He was asked to consider taking on a very dangerous job—to serve Israel as a spy in an Arab country.

The agent explained to Cohen further that his family would be well taken care of and that, if he agreed to take on the job, he should understand that his principal reward would be in knowing that he was carrying out a mission for Israel that could help save hundreds, perhaps even thousands, of Israeli lives.

He was advised to think it over, and under no circumstances to discuss the conversation with anyone. The agent also stated very clearly to Cohen that the risks of being a spy were great and that, if he were caught, the chances of his being executed were very high.

Eli Cohen did not take very much time to consider the offer. He let the agent know that he was prepared to undertake the assignment. It was decided that his wife should be told that he was being sent abroad to carry out important business missions for Israel and that these trips made it difficult to communicate regularly. She acknowledged the explanation, although it is conceivable that in her heart of hearts she suspected that her husband was undertaking a secret, dangerous mission for Israel. She knew how much he loved his new country.

For the next several months, Eli Cohen lived undercover somewhere in Israel and was taught how to operate a secret radio transmitter, how to code and decipher messages, what kinds of military information to look for. His assignment was Syria, which at the time was in control of the Golan Heights overlooking Israel's Galilee region, from which there was an almost never-ending barrage of artillery fire, as well as terrorist attacks on isolated settlements. The Israelis felt they had to know much more about the military situation in that area in case there should be an outbreak of fighting, as most of their intelligence people suspected would happen sooner or later.

Eli Cohen was shipped off to Argentina, which has a large Arab community, and began to live a double life. He posed as an Arab businessman, made friends with the military attaché of the Syrian Embassy, and generally let it be known that he was a successful young executive who also enjoyed the pleasures of life. He was a free spender, inviting his new friends to dinners and parties, and soon became well known and well liked. He was known now as Kamal Tabas.

Some time later he returned to the Middle East, specifically to Damascus, Syria's capital, which is relatively close to Israel. He rented an expensive apartment, installed his secret radio transmitter, and began to broaden his circle of friends and acquaintances in the ruling circles of the country, especially the military.

His lavish home became a center for parties where Syrian military and government officials found a warm host whose bar seemed constantly well stocked, where they could meet attractive, exciting people from the world of the theater and art, and they always seemed to have a very good time. Of course, only Eli Cohen / Kamal Tabas knew that in the ceiling of the apartment, only a few feet from where the parties took place, there was concealed a secret radio transmitter which the Israeli agent used almost daily to provide information that he hoped would eventually enable the Israeli military intelligence to know in depth and in detail the exact strength of various units of the Syrian armed forces, their locations and capabilities, and their tactical and strategic plans.

For long stretches of time, Eli Cohen did not communicate directly with his family, and left it to his superiors to explain his absence as best they could. During the time that he carried out his assignment—a matter of years—there can be little doubt that he was terribly lonesome for his wife and children, and for Israel itself. The constant threat of exposure and execution must surely have kept him in a state of high tension; but throughout the time he was a spy, he never let it show, not to his friends in Syria nor to his superiors in Israel. It seems that he had been almost born to the job.

He learned how to pretend to be a heavy drinker, and listened carefully when guests in his home who had been drinking too much began to talk of military information. He remembered every detail, and when his guests finally left, he would spring into action, first making notes and then transcribing the information into code, and finally broadcasting it to Tel Aviv, at a specific time on a special radio band. He felt that every bit of information he passed to Israel was another powerful weapon in helping to defend the country.

After a while top Syrian military officials began to invite him to their Damascus headquarters, where they actually let him look at classified documents, trusting him implicitly. At one time, Cohen/Tabas was even invited to broadcast a special radio program from Syria to the Arab community in South America, relaying official government propaganda—which he proceeded to do, urging his "Arab brothers" over the seas to support the Syrian government.

In all, he remained in Syria for three years, and during that time managed to visit Israel and his family for brief periods, doing so through circuitous routes and disguises. One of the early pieces of information he brought with him to Israel was specific planning on Syria's part to divert the essential waters of the Baniyas River so as to dry up Israel's chief water source, the Sea of Galilee and the Jordan River. Efforts by the Syrians to implement the plan were blocked by the Israelis' accurate artillery fire that pinpointed and then destroyed their efforts.

He became a frequent visitor to the Syrian-Israeli border, at the invitation of high Syrian military officials, and would look, observe carefully, and soon transmit everything that he had seen. The information that was thus assembled helped the Israelis immeasurably when the 1967 Six Day War erupted and the Syrians were driven back from their positions on the Golan Heights.

In 1964 Cohen's radio signals were found to be interfering with official transmitters located in the Syrian military compound nearby. His transmitter was traced, and his true identity was discovered. The black moment that Cohen had undoubtedly always feared had indeed arrived. The Syrian counterintelligence people who now crowded into Cohen's apartment, where his secret radio was discovered, at first assumed that he was an Arab traitor. When the truth emerged that he was a Jew from Israel, they could not bring themselves to believe it.

On the day of his capture Cohen was forced to

transmit a false message to Tel Aviv to confuse the Israelis. However, he sent the message at a slower speed than was normal, which was the signal to his superiors in Israel that he had been apprehended, and they discarded the incorrect message sent— and realized that the time for tears for their man in Syria would soon arrive.

For a while, when it became known that an Israeli spy had been captured in Damascus, panic swept over the city. Hundreds of people were arrested on suspicion of collaboration, but eventually things quieted down, and a trial took place in February 1965.

No foreign newsmen were allowed into the courtroom, but at one point General Al-Hafez, who had questioned Cohen, said of the spy, "He conducted himself in a very brave and honorable fashion during a most trying experience."

At the trial, when he was asked to identify himself, Cohen said, "I am Eli Cohen, Israeli soldier."

He was sentenced to hang, and the execution took place after midnight. His body was left dangling in the public square, wrapped m a large sheet of paper on which was scrawled, "Eli Cohen was sentenced to death in the name of the Arab people of Syria after being found guilty of delivering secret information to the enemy." Thousands of people who could not come to the square saw the dangling body on Syrian television.

The request of Eli Cohen's family that his body

be returned to Israel for burial was refused. In Israel tens of thousands of Jews mourned the loss of a man who had given up his life willingly to help defend the country he loved.

In Jerusalem, Israel's capital, a street has been named for him. His story has become a glowing chapter in the history of the young nation.

MARK SPITZ
Olympic Champion

WHEN HE WAS ONLY TEN years old, Mark Spitz won his first award for swimming. He knew from that moment on that he would attempt to become one of the great swimmers of the world.

He was born in California in 1950, but when he was only two his parents moved to Hawaii, a swimmers' paradise. He spent many days at the famed Waikiki Beach, dashing into the water without fear, seeming to find himself in his true element. A few years later the family returned to California, and Mark continued his swimming practice and began to study swimming from professional instructors.

He attended religious school and was bar mitzvah. By the time Mark was fourteen, the great swimming coach George Haines predicted that he would become one of the greatest swimmers of all time. People used to line up at indoor and outdoor pools to watch him flit by in the water at unbelievable speeds.

In 1967 the magazine *Swimming World* named him the Swimmer of the Year. That was the year that he had broken three American and five world records, and had also won five gold medals in the Pan-American games held in Canada.

The next year he entered the Olympics, held in Mexico. He was superbly confident of his skill and was sure he would win six gold medals, but only managed to capture two. The next year he went to Israel, where he entered the Maccabiah, the sporting event held every four years for Jewish athletes from all parts of the world. He walked off with four gold medals.

When the 1972 Olympics were announced in Munich, he was a leading entry, although he knew that overconfidence could cost him dearly. A seasoned, experienced swimmer by now and a wiser contestant, he said little and made up his mind to do his best.

The first race he entered was a tough one: the 200-meter butterfly contest, which called for strenuous strokes; he won his first gold medal at Munich. The next day there was a 400-meter freestyle relay race, and again he walked off with a gold medal. The next day he won yet another gold medal; in three days, he had already accumulated five gold medals at the Olympics, and still there remained two more races to enter. In quick succession, as though he were more a creature of the sea than a human being, he completed both races successfully, winning two more gold medals, for a total of seven—a record that has not been beaten.

His achievement was incredible: He was not only the first person in Olympics history to win seven gold medals in swimming but the first person to win seven gold medals in any sporting event in the Olympics. He was honored by all lovers of sports the world over, and was named Male Athlete of the Year by the Associated Press.

The victory at Munich was marred for Spitz, however, by the murder of a group of Israeli athletes by Arab terrorists. People throughout the world were shocked and grieved by the attack, but Mark Spitz was especially stirred.

After his return home to California and the first few weeks and months of basking in the limelight of worldwide publicity for his stunning achievements, he seemed to take a new and more serious attitude toward his Jewish background. He loved swimming, of course, but it seemed as though he suddenly came to the realization that zooming through the water at breakneck speeds was not the only worthwhile thing he wanted to do with his life.

Mark Spitz decided that he would use his new fame to help causes and programs that he felt keenly about, and for the past number of years he could be found delivering speeches to groups of Jewish students and to various organizational meetings, urging that they support the needs of Israel and take a deeper interest in their own Jewish heritage and background.

Only time will tell if anyone will ever again match or top the incredible successes that he piled up at the Olympics in Munich.

JAN PEERCE
Lower East Side to the Met

JACOB PINCUS PERELMUTH, better known as
the world acclaimed operatic tenor Jan Peerce,
was born in 1904 in a coldwater apartment on the
Lower East Side of New York. His early years
were very difficult, and he never forgot them. He
has evolved into a compassionate friend of all
people in need.

As a young student, the field of medicine appealed to him, but then he discovered that music
was even more important to him than the art of
healing. He learned to play the violin, and played
for many years with a dance orchestra. Occasionally he would sing; gradually it dawned on him
that he was blessed with a remarkable voice, and
he concentrated on a singing career.

The late great conductor Arturo Toscanini heard
him sing at Radio City Music Hall and signed him

to a long-term contract as soloist with the new NBC Symphony Orchestra. A few years later Jan Peerce made his debut as an opera singer, and by 1941 he was the leading tenor in the Metropolitan Opera's production of *La Traviata*.

Peerce never shies away from letting his audiences know that he was once an impoverished Jewish boy brought up in the tenements of New York. He has delighted concert and opera audiences throughout the world, and through television has come to be known and admired by millions of people for his sensitive interpretations of classical operatic works.

One of the roles that he played with special effectiveness was that of Tevye in the highly successful *Fiddler on the Roof*. Peerce is an observant, committed Jew, who delights in singing cantorial works, Hebrew and Yiddish songs, and the role of the poor but wise milkman in the Shalom Aleichem classic seemed almost custom-made for him.

He has performed in Israel many times, frequently donating his fees to various welfare institutions. When he travels, he often takes along canned fish and other preserved food since he is meticulous about the observance of *kashrut*. He likes to tell the story of the time he was visiting in Moscow, where he was scheduled to sing. He was in his hotel room early in the morning and had put on his *tefillin*, when the Russian maid entered the room, saw him preparing to place a large *tallit* or prayer shawl around his shoulders, and went screaming from the room. She was convinced that something demonic was about to take place.

When his late brother-in-law, Richard Tucker, the noted Metropolitan star, was alive, the two would often harmonize, enjoying especially renditions of nostalgic old Yiddish folk songs. In 1977 the America-Israel Cultural Foundation presented him with its Tarbut-Culture Medal, for his "outstanding, diversified and continuing contribution to the cultural life of all people."

In his autobiography, *The Bluebird of Happiness*, Peerce continued to express his wonder at the fact that a youngster from the slums of New York could rise to become one of the world's best-loved and acclaimed performers. He died in 1984.

HERBERT H. LEHMAN
Conscience of the Senate

HE WAS BORN with the proverbial spoon in his mouth but from an early age displayed a sincere, deep interest in the welfare of people less fortunate than himself. When he died, he was mourned by all Americans, for he had brought to his role as a public servant a rare combination of compassion and toughness.

Herbert Lehman was born in New York in 1878, the son of a wealthy German Jewish immigrant who had established a major investment house and who had been one of the founders of the Cotton Exchange in New York. After graduating from college, young Lehman would travel from his family's comfortable home in the upper part of New York to the Lower East Side to work as a volunteer with the Henry Street Settlement, where he personally ministered to the needs of the poor

181

and the ill. He never said it in words, but it was clear to all those who worked alongside him that he enjoyed performing these acts of kindness.

At a later date he was persuaded to enter the family's banking and textile businesses, but after serving on a commission to revise the existing banking laws, he realized that he could be more effective in aiding the needy through politics than through banking, and in 1928 he was elected lieutenant governor of New York, serving alongside the governor, Franklin D. Roosevelt. When Roosevelt became President in 1932, Lehman became governor and was re-elected four times. His record as a devoted executive profoundly interested in the welfare of all the people made him one of the most popular governors in the country. Other states began to copy the models of labor reform, protection of the aged and the young, and the laws against religious and social discrimination that he instituted and carried out.

President Roosevelt, even before the Second World War ended in 1945, designated him to lead a special worldwide relief and rehabilitation organization that was established to ameliorate the suffering of millions of people in war-ravaged countries. The agency eventually became the UNRRA, attached to the United Nations, and Lehman ran it with exemplary success and outstanding results.

In the period immediately after the end of the

war, Lehman devoted considerable time and effort to aiding the United Jewish Appeal amass the many millions of dollars needed to aid the Jews who had survived the Holocaust and to help in the plans for creating a Jewish homeland. He had been one of the leaders of the Joint Distribution Committee for many years, which was set up after the end of the First World War to aid the uprooted and impoverished Jewish communities.

In 1949 Lehman was elected to the United States Senate, where he soon became known as the "conscience of the Senate." He led in strong support for the State of Israel, and was a leader of the small progressive body of liberal senators who battled against the era of McCarthyism that had overtaken the country. He remained an influential leader in the Democratic party after he left the Senate, and died in 1963, assured that he had made the world a little better than when he had first entered it.

AHARON
SHEAR-YASHUV
From Convert to Rabbi

MOST JEWS ARE BORN into the Jewish community. But some become Jews, abandoning their original religious persuasion, out of the conviction that Judaism offers them a more rewarding, meaningful way of life.

Traditionally, Judaism has been opposed to seeking converts, but when a person from another faith has shown a genuine desire to be part of the Jewish community and has conformed to the rules governing such a conversion, he has been accepted wholly and fully as a Jew with equal rights and obligations with all other Jews. One of the most famous converts, of course, is the biblical Ruth, great-grandmother of King David. Scattered through the United States, Israel, and other coun-

185

tries today are several thousands of recent converts, who have chosen to become part and parcel of the Jewish people.

One of the most unusual and remarkable such converts is a rabbi now living in Haifa, Israel. His new name is Aharon Shear-Yashuv, and to look at him one would never guess that he was once a German Christian. The *yarmulke* never leaves his head, a full beard girdles his face, and as the rabbi-in-residence of an Israeli university he is kept busy advising students, teaching, leading services, and supervising and conducting marriages, circumcisions, bar mitzvah ceremonies, and other events.

The story begins in Germany soon after the end of World War II, when he was a small child. All around him there was gloom and depression as the German people sought to reconstruct their lives after the black years of the Nazi era and their defeat by the Allies in one of the cruelest wars in history. The young man's father was believed to have been sympathetic to the Nazi movement, but at that time there was no talk of this.

He grew up in a small town, was a good student, and decided to become a lawyer. Once in the university, however, he found himself drawn to studies of philosophy and religion, and soon he began to take as many courses as he could in theology. He took a special interest in Judaism, and one of his professors recommended that he continue his studies at the Hebrew Union College in Cincinnati, a rabbinical seminary for Reform rabbis which offered nonrabbinical students an opportunity to study Judaism on a graduate level.

At the Cincinnati campus, the young German student involved himself deeply in his studies. He learned Hebrew, Talmud, Jewish mysticism, and history, and gradually it dawned on him that he was moving toward conversion to Judaism. He met frequently with his academic advisors and with various scholars, and finally decided that, as much as he liked the Cincinnati institution, he had a feeling that he was learning a watered-down version of Judaism since It was Reform-oriented. He made up his mind that the only place for him to learn the authentic forms of Judaism was in Jerusalem, and in an Orthodox school.

He proceeded to Jerusalem and was enrolled in a yeshiva of higher learning. He had by this time mastered Hebrew and Aramaic well enough to be able to study Talmud in the original. He was a model student, often surpassing many of the Jewish students in his zeal and comprehension. The aura of Jerusalem, and of Israel itself, had a great influence over him. From time to time he would visit the Yad Vashem, an imposing memorial for the Jews who perished in the Holocaust.

Finally he announced that he planned to become a Jew, and after he was examined, challenged, and interviewed, he was accepted and underwent all the rituals of formal conversion. His mother and sister in Germany accepted his decision, but his father broke off all contact with him. After years of intensive study and training, he was ordained a rabbi in Jerusalem, and later was appointed as rabbi of the Technion-Israel Institute of Technology in Haifa, which has a student body of about nine thousand.

Rabbi Aharon Shear-Yashuv married a *sabra* (native-born Israeli) girl and they have three children. Students and visitors to the Technion campus who attend services at the institute's synagogue enjoy his sermons, as well as the classes he teaches to students and faculty members. They come to him for counseling as they would to any rabbi.

Occasionally Rabbi Shear-Yashuv visits his family in Germany, and he especially likes staying at his sister's home because it is within walking distance of a small traditional synagogue. One of the tasks he feels most keenly about is introducing recently arrived Soviet Jewish students to the fundamentals of Judaism. With barely a smile, he explains, "They were cut off from our heritage for more than half a century, and it is a *mitzvah* of the highest priority to reintroduce them to the fountains of our tradition."

HENRIETTA SZOLD
Savior of the Children

A SMALL, white-haired woman of eighty-five died in Jerusalem a few years before the establishment of Israel, and a whole generation of Jews mourned for her. She had devoted her life to the welfare of her people, saving thousands, encouraging tens of thousands, and inspiring hundreds of thousands. Her name was Henrietta Szold.

The daughter of a rabbi and scholar, she was born in Baltimore in 1860 and although few girls in those days received more than a nominal Jewish education, Henrietta was an exception—her father taught her Hebrew, Bible, Talmud, Jewish history, and the great texts of Jewish literature. She became a teacher in a Baltimore girls' school and also taught religious classes in the synagogue school.

In the 1880s, following an outbreak of pogroms in czarist Russia, Jewish refugees began to stream

189

into Baltimore, and she decided she wanted to help them personally. She conceived the idea of a night school where adults could study English and the rudiments of American life, and before long her idea became a reality and she became one of the teachers of the newcomers. The plight of the refugees, the problems they encountered of adjusting to a totally new life, and the knowledge that there remained in faroff Europe many hundreds of thousands of other Jews still living miserable lives under the domination of despotic governments made her decide that she would devote herself to helping her fellow Jews.

One area she felt was vital was the lack of English-language translations of the great Jewish classics, and so she set about translating a number of works, including the multivolume *Legends of the Jews* by Louis Ginsberg. To further this end, she went to work for the Jewish Publication Society in Philadelphia, seeking to open up the great Jewish literary treasures to a largely English-speaking Jewish community in America.

Soon after the turn of the century, at the age of forty-three, she moved to New York and enrolled as a student at the Jewish Theological Seminary, the only woman in an all-male rabbinical seminary. She explained that she was driven by a desire to learn and to share that learning with all who were interested. A few years later, having adopted the Zionist program launched by Theodor Herzl in

Europe, she set sail for Palestine to see for herself that strip of land that she knew only from reading. When she returned to New York, a woman already in her fifties, she was determined that something had to be done to provide medical help for the Jews and the Arabs in Palestine: She had seen the ravages of malaria and trachoma and the absence of elementary hygiene standards, and she sensed that this was the challenge that had been awaiting her all her life.

On Purim, the festival that celebrates the victory of Queen Esther over the wicked Haman, who planned to murder all the Jews in the ancient Persian Empire, Henrietta Szold told a group of women in a Jewish study circle, "If we are Zionists, as we say we are, what is the good of meeting and talking and drinking tea? Let us do something real and practical—let us organize the Jewish women of America and send nurses and doctors to Palestine." The suggestion caught fire, and then and there a new organization was born, Hadassah, which is the Hebrew name for Queen Esther.

Henrietta Szold became the first president of the group, and the first step planned was to send two nurses to Jerusalem to heal the sick and to teach the fundamental laws of health. Six years later, when World War I was ended, a whole medical unit organized by Hadassah set sail for Palestine, consisting of forty-four people, including physicians, nurses, and public health specialists, and equipment for a fifty-bed hospital. Since that time, Hadassah has grown into an organization of 350,000 women who have provided vast amounts of medical care for hundreds of thousands of Jewish and non-Jewish patients alike, first in Palestine and now in Israel. The Hadassah Medical Center in Jerusalem is considered one of the greatest lifesaving institutions in the world.

Like many other people, Miss Szold, who settled in Palestine in the 1920s, had believed that the year 1918 marked the end of all wars, but of course the rise of Nazism changed her thinking. Early in the 1930s, soon after the persecution of the Jews in Germany began, she and others set up a massive rescue program for young people whose parents were unable to leave Germany. The program, called Youth Aliyah, eventually brought tens of thousands of German (and later Austrian) Jewish youths to Palestine.

Whenever a ship bringing a new contingent of these Youth Aliyah immigrants arrived at Haifa, Henrietta Szold was on the dock, waiting to greet them and help them in their first difficult months of adjustment to a new life—just as she had done so many years ago as a young woman in her native Baltimore. She wrote once that as the years of World War II progressed, the children reaching Palestine as Youth Aliyah wards seemed to change: "They seemed to become more sick, more bitter, without hope for the future. . . . It took months of patient effort for our social workers and nurses and doctors to restore their self-confidence, and to give them back their hope in the future."

Although in her earlier years she had translated more than ten books from German and Hebrew and had been an active collaborator in the publication of the *Jewish Encyclopedia,* which appeared in 1905, she was now no longer interested in anything except the saving of lives.

She also saw in Hadassah's major medical and health programs in Palestine an opportunity to build a bridge between the Jews and the Arabs. In a letter to her sister, Bertha, prior to the establishment of Israel in 1948, she wrote:

> You know the Arabs are using violence and terror to stop us. They even killed two Hadassah nurses on their way to take care of Arab patients.... I warned our young people to use self-control whenever there is a clash between Jews and Arabs. ... We hope for friendship with our Arab neighbors, we want to develop the country for the good of both the Jews and the Arabs.... We do not know what the future will bring but we pray and work for healing and peace.

Tens of thousands of young Israelis are still receiving help from the Youth Aliyah organization, only now they are not being rescued from

Nazi Germany but are being taken from environments which have turned them into criminals and delinquents and are being given a chance to rehabilitate themselves. Tens of thousands of middle-aged Israelis who reached the shores of Palestine in the years before the outbreak of World War II in 1939 look upon Miss Szold as a true guardian angel.

And in America, in the same spirit of resolve and dedication, vast numbers of Hadassah members and their families press forward in the work of healing and rescue that Henrietta Szold first conceived when she saw the victims of czarist tyranny arrive in Baltimore in the latter part of the nineteenth century.

Is it any wonder that Henrietta Szold, who herself never married, has nevertheless been called a veritable matriarch of Israel in our own time?